bedr

A BEGINNER'S GUIDE

C000212920

PIPER TERRETT

bedroom DJ

A BEGINNER'S GUIDE

PIPER TERRETT

OMNIBUS PRESS

London/New York/Paris/Sydney/Copenhagen/Berlin/Madrid/Tokyo

ISBN: 0.7119.9765.9
Order No: OP 49368

Exclusive Distributors:
Music Sales Limited,
8/9 Frith Street,
London W1D 3JB, UK.

Music Sales Corporation,
257 Park Avenue South,
New York, NY 10010, USA.

Macmillan Distribution Services,
53 Park West Drive,
Derrimut, Vic 3030,
Australia.

To the Music Trade only:
Music Sales Limited,
8/9 Frith Street,
London W1D 3JB, UK.

Typeset by Galleon Typesetting, Ipswich
Printed in Great Britain by Cox & Wyman Ltd, Reading, Berks.

A catalogue record for this book is available from the British Library.

Visit Omnibus Press on the web at www.omnibuspress.com

For my parents Helen and David Terrett:

'She who dares spins'

To HARLAN
From Dad
12th JANUARY 06.

Contents

Foreword

by Tony Prince

In 1964, about a year after I'd introduced The Beatles on stage the night they went to number one for the first time, I was expelled from the Musicians Union because they didn't like me playing records in the Bristol Top Rank. I was a singer/guitarist with the 16-piece band and when they had a break I played the records for a bit of extra cash. Now it was over – I became a DJ because Rank paid me money to be their scapegoat for the rule "Keep Music Live". I have always missed my career as a musician even though the most fun filled part of my life was as a DJ (1966–68) on Radio Caroline, the pirate radio ship.

I first spotted the potential of mixing back in 1981. I'd been with Radio Luxembourg 14 years by then and had become Programme Director. This meant I could continue DJing and select the music for Europe's largest ever radio station (at its peak the English Service had 50 million UK and European listeners). This also meant I selected the DJs to work on the station and I'm afraid I was responsible for giving their first national radio breaks to Mike Reed, Steve Wright and . . . Timmy Mallet! (I do apologise). One day a tape arrived on my desk together with the hundred tapes that arrived each week from wannabe 208 Radio Luxembourg DJs. This DJ didn't talk after the records but rather mixed them into a beautiful non-stop medley. I invited the young Welsh DJ to do a weekly mix for me which I broadcast in my weekly dance music show. The response was sensational but the main thrust of mail was penned by . . . DJs. DJs who wanted to know, "How can I get hold of those mixes to play in my club?" or "How can I learn to mix?" or "Please find enclosed MY mix for your show." And so we launched mixing records as an art form. The Technics SL1200 turntable became a musical instrument. Sampling devices arrived and the word mixing metamorphosised into 'remixing'.

Thoroughly convinced that I could make a success of a DJ *only* record label, backed by the music industry, my wife Christine and I threw our lives behind the Disco Mix Club. As well as providing DJs with exclusive mix creations, we also sent them a new magazine which we christened *Mixmag*. With the power of the press to influence our direction, we took the DJs on a musical ride that would change dance music and the DJs potential as a producer/musician forever.

Along the way key DJs influenced and directed the art. Sanny-X from Sweden blew everyone away with his wild edits and complete originality and was the first DJ to chart with a 'bedroom' remix of Tina Charles' 'I Love To Love'. Les Adams [see chapter 9], who we managed, became the first UK DJ to chart in his own right as LA Mix. We launched the DMC TECHNICS WORLD DJ CHAMPIONSHIPS which brought remixing to a live arena. Chad Jackson was our first British winner and went on to chart big time with another bedroom mix, 'Hear The Drummer Get Wicked'.

Bedroom DJing has become the world's biggest musical hobby. It frightens many people in the music industry but to those of us who like the idea that music should run free like water, it's a 21st Century concept all right. Don't get me wrong, the main artery of music should be protected least we sink to a sample, we need the stars, heroes and icons and the big, expensive productions. But there's room for free music too and I believe bedroom mixing is something to be excited about –

10

track sharing, discussing ideas and concepts. It's a much better hobby than clog dancing!

DJing has long been a male dominated activity and it's great to see more women coming through and challenging the boys at their game. From big names like Lottie and Sister Bliss to those like Piper Terrett, just tentatively starting out. This book is a tribute to those bedroom DJs everywhere, whatever their sex.

Come and meet thousands of DJs and bedroom mixers in DJPAGES on our **dmcworld.com** web site. Let's get down to making music and not war!

Tony Prince.

(Founder of DMC – the worldwide DJ organisation
and chairman of World DJ Fund for Music Therapy)

Introduction

It all began on a Saturday afternoon much like any other. I pottered about Oxford Street in the mid-September sunshine, dodging the beautiful young things in their low-slung hipster jeans, and the exhibitionist couples holding hands as the girlfriends attempted simultaneously to snog and rubber neck the shop window of Karen Millen. There I was, at the tender age of five and twenty years already a bitter and twisted spinster, whiling away my weekend with the customary short-lived thrills of retail therapy. My hypochondriac heart still ached from the torments of a brief love affair with a bedroom DJ who had recently dumped me to spend more time with his record collection. The only, albeit temporary, respite from such ills seemed to be found in purchasing tight-fitting outfits from Hennes and scouring Berwick Street's record shops for vinyl I could not play. Heartbreak was turning me into a bizarre hybrid of Bridget Jones and that vinyl junkie dropout Rob from *High Fidelity*. I didn't own a record player, but even if I had had one at this early stage in my music career I would not have known how to switch it on. I was a terminal technophobe who could barely change a lightbulb let alone programme the video. Despite these grave obstacles some tiny part of my brain had begun to insist that somehow my future lay amongst the dusty second-hand vinyl stores of Soho, and those mystical hi-fi labels, Vestax and Gemini.

My spiritual transition from DJ cast-off to L-plated turntablist in my own right – my "Road to Ibiza" conversion if you like –

had happened one night at Metrogroove at Turnmills about a month previously and took me completely by surprise. An unexotic location you might say, compared with that of Saul trotting along the A-road to Damascus, but a similarly life changing experience. I was dancing away to Danny Rampling, minding my own business amongst the sweat and sleazy guys when I saw a poster on the wall declaiming that someone called Lottie was going to be playing there. No bloke would call himself Lottie, surely? They were always called DJ Bonecrusher or DJ Sexy Beast – never something as unpretentious as just "Lottie", so she must be female. Was it possible that women could be DJs, I wondered in my crushing ignorance.

Over the period of about two hours the crazy idea began to dawn on me that if someone called Lottie could play at Turnmills then why couldn't I learn to spin some tunes? I had some cash – I'd get my own decks and learn to do it in my bedroom. I had a vague idea of what you needed to get – I'd seen my ex play on his decks enough times and had helped carry his mixer down the stairs once so I knew what one looked like. If my evil ex could do it, then why couldn't I? After all, he might have been technologically minded, but he was tone deaf and couldn't hold a tune in a bucket. Gradually the mad idea I thought would sound ridiculous during my post-Turnmills hangover began to make more and more sense. I spent hours at work diligently trawling the internet for equipment shops when I was meant to be researching the stock market. Slowly I mastered the important distinction between direct drive and belt drive turntables. I even bought *DJ Magazine* and left it lying around the flat to impress my flatmate Nina. Of course as a financial journalist I would ensure I got expert advice before buying equipment and spend time looking for the best deal. Oh yeah.

A month later as I trudged along on that fateful Saturday afternoon, I remember my feet suddenly quickening at the thought of the electrical delights awaiting me in the emporia of Tottenham Court Road. Before long I stood pressing my nose against the warm glass of the hi-fi shop windows, whispering that hallowed name over and over again. . . . Technics. The next thing I knew I was in the back seat of a recklessly driven minicab, *en route* home to North London with a set of spankingly new record decks in the boot, an amp and a mixer. And worse, much worse than that – they were brand new Technics SL1210s (Mark 2). I trembled in my trainers at the sacrilegious thought of me, a mere beginner and – horror of horrors – *female* at that, splashing out on the tool of the professional DJ. What's more, I had walked off the street and in record time even for me succeeded in spending a thousand pounds I didn't have in less than ten minutes. If I listened carefully enough I could hear the long-suffering credit card in my wallet gently weeping. Hazily, I recall standing at the shop counter as I sacrificed the plastic, half expecting the sales advisor to sneer that they only sold equipment to genuine DJs, not their vindictive ex-girlfriends who couldn't tell a crossfader from a croissant. Who the devil did I think I was and what the bloody hell would my mum/boss/flatmate/cat think when they found out? Sinking back into the passenger seat, I hung my head in shame. *What had I done?*

1

Getting Tooled Up

Shit. *Shit. SHIT.* I'd really done it this time. My foolish pipe dream of learning to DJ had quickly turned into a twisted metal nightmare on the living room carpet. Microscopic screws were hiding in the shag pile, record needles lay abandoned amongst the cold takeaway pizza, and miscellaneous bolts crunched under my slippers as I sat holding my head in my hands. This irresistible urge overcame me – the sudden desire to take my half-built Technics record decks and throw them violently against the wall, screaming blue DJ murder at the top of my voice. A sort of post-modern tribute to The Who. Maybe the real reason Pete Townshend *et al.* smashed up their stuff was because they had trouble restringing a guitar, only it wasn't hip to admit it. If only I were Björk I could record it all, play it backwards and then make it into some weird Techno track. Tracy Emin could display the smashed fragments of the turntables on a background of soiled underpants and tampons in the Tate Modern and call it *Failed Female DJ.* Now I understood how Dad felt that New Year's Eve in 1984 when he stamped on his brand new digital watch because he couldn't change the year, or read the Japanese instruction manual. I had dutifully studied the Technics manual in minute detail but still couldn't make the damn things work.

Just in time I remembered the new £890 balance on my

plastic. Are credit card purchases insured against consumer rage, I wondered? Another question. *Why exactly* did I want to be a DJ, again? Someone please remind me because right now the reasoning utterly escapes me. I thought all you had to do was buy the right equipment, plug it in and switch it on. No bugger told me I'd fork out a thousand quid and then have to build the bloody thing myself. What did they think this was? The Ministry of Sound's answer to the *Krypton Factor*? Ha bloody ha. How come learning to DJ meant you somehow had to become an engineer overnight? There was nothing in any of the glossy DJing magazines about this. No stories of Timo Maas struggling to put his turntables together, no gossip on it all going Pete Tong on Boy George as he tries to adjust a tone arm for the first time. Oh no. It was all slick, cool, hip and trendy – and in that order, schweetie. All geeky guys in *Carhartt* T-shirts and baseball caps looking nonchalantly away from the camera as they discussed their latest stint in the recording studio, *man*, talked about *the scene* and their favourite brand of weed. Right then a joint would probably have done me some good, but being a total square my lifelong drug of choice was and always would be a strong cup of PG.

Maybe this was why guys were DJs and birds were told to stick to hobbies like knitting and trying to lose weight. After all, us girls knew it was blokes that liked fiddling with bits of metal – that is, when they weren't fiddling with themselves. I'd overstepped the mark big time, been taken well and truly for a mug and would be forced to retreat to my former pastimes of amateur tarot reading (I hadn't predicted this outcome, surprise, surprise) and slagging off my ex-boyfriend (I was up to PhD level on this subject). The assistant in the dodgy fly-by-night electrical shop I'd patronised earlier in the day was no doubt sitting at home sinking the Saturday night beers with his mates and laughing about what a 24 carat plonker he'd taken me for.

Let me set the scene. After my impulsive purchase, I'd arrived back home guiltily to my scabby little flat, my head spinning but relieved that my flatmate Nina was away for the weekend and wouldn't be able to lecture me on what a waste of money it all was. We were moving house in about a month's time and I had promised faithfully to wait until we were safely settled in the new flat before splashing out on bulky DJing equipment which would only get in the way. Only, predictably greedy guts couldn't wait. That evening I couldn't sit still until I'd torn open the boxes of all my equipment and had a good look at everything. Unfortunately I wasn't too sure what it all was or was supposed to do. The mixer was in one piece and looked reasonably straightforward enough, but the turntables came in complicated bits incased in bubble wrap. These things called headshells – tiny, fiddly little bastards – were apparently meant to hold the record needles in place and attach to the record arm, but the screws to fit them kept disappearing up my fingernails. As I couldn't find a screwdriver I was forced to use a kitchen knife instead and it took me an hour to tighten the first screw. My mate Maxine rang up and I chatted away to her as I attempted to attach these microscopic coloured leads to points inside the equally minuscule headshell. It was only a matter of time before one of the leads came away in my hand. AAAAGGHGHGHHGH!

Defeat overcame me in my exhaustion and I wept into my copy of *Jockey Slut*. At the very first hurdle, I had failed my initiation into the secret world of the Disc Jockey. Through the pain, the misery and the hot tears which seemed to taste of tea I threw a despairing glance across the room at the half-built record player balancing precariously on the coffee table. It was then that I noticed the strange looking plugs. They had only two prongs. Surely that wasn't right? I couldn't remember much from my Dad's lessons on changing a plug but I knew there were meant to be three. And why was it that most of the manual seemed to be written in German? My heart sank into my slippers. I'd been diddled, hadn't I? I'd spent all that money on grey imports from Transylvania or somewhere that I couldn't even plug in and play if I did complete the Herculean task of putting them together. I'd have more luck building turntables out of toilet rolls *à la Blue Peter*. Stifling the sobs, I shut the living room door carefully behind me and ran to Maxine's house before I did any more permanent damage to the equipment or my mental health.

On reflection I had been a complete muppet in my approach to buying equipment. In the back of my mind there had been the nagging thought that I should get proper expert advice before splashing out on the wrong thing, but as usual excitement and greed had overwhelmed me and I bought the first set of decks I laid eyes on in my rush to get them home. I had a vague idea that Technics were supposed to be a good brand – a couple of mates had assured me so – but that was all I knew. I decided that it would be a good idea to get hold of a real professional DJ and corner him in a cafe for a couple of hours until he told me everything I wanted to know about equipment purchases. After all, if he didn't know what to buy then who would? Music magazines were full of interviews with celebrity DJs but they never told beginners what they really wanted to know – like where did they buy their first set of decks and what problems did they encounter with them? I decided that Ali B would be a good candidate. He's resident DJ at Fabric, has been DJing for eight years and also has a show on Capital Radio, so he knows his stuff. I caught up with him in the Dome cafe in Islington and asked him to explain a few technical fundamentals. In my case it was shutting the door after the horse had bolted but maybe I could learn a thing or two to stand me in good stead in the future. Incidentally, he is no relative of Ali G!

PT: *How old were you when you started to DJ?*

AB: Probably about seventeen or eighteen. But before that I was an avid music collector from the age of ten. You know, I'd just chase down certain tracks. You hear an artist and you want to know more about them. I was buying 7 inches and cassettes – CDs weren't out and about at that point. I started off just collecting records really and then I bought a deck. Well, I had kind of loads of hi-fi bits really but I bought a deck from a car boot sale for about £4. That was my first proper deck. It had a steel base with a little pitch control on it. I used the pitch to change the speed of the records. So yeah it just started from there really. I used to mix to the radio when I started off because I only had one deck.

PT: *So you really started out with a deck worth £4?!*

AB: Well I think it cost about £4.80! It was from a hospital car boot sale. Me and a mate had been up all night and rolled past it in the morning and just kind of saw it. I've still got it now actually – it was a really good deck. What you've got to make sure is that you've got something that's sturdy, so you can't have a deck that is sprung obviously because it'll just bounce around. Something with a steel base, with a pretty good pickup, so that when you let go of the record the beat'll reach its correct speed immediately. If it takes a while to go 'wwuuuuuhhhh' that's not what you want.

PT: *You mean, direct drive?*

AB: Direct drive. Pitch control. My first deck had just plus 3 and minus 3 on it and the same kind of layout as a Technics 1210. So I got that and a cheap mixer – just literally something that you could bring two channels in at once – it wasn't really a proper mixer. I think it had a crossfader on it, I can't remember. And then because I only had one deck I just put records on and listened to the radio and when there was something I could mix to I'd go to a record, start the beat mixing and just get used to counting the beats.

PT: *What advice would you give on buying equipment?*

AB: OK, obviously you need a good amp and speakers – that's just a good investment. You can do anything with it, you can put anything through it. You can run your television through it, you can put your tape through it, whatever. You know you want to have speakers which are clear because you've got to be able to listen to the sound when you're mixing but that's not essential. Any amp and speakers will do. You can pick them up second-hand for £30 for an amp, £20, you know it's irrelevant what you have, it's just your budget. The most important thing is the decks.

PT: *What sort of decks should beginners buy?*

AB: There are hundreds on the market but the industry standard are Technics 1210s and there isn't really any point in getting anything less than a 1210. A 1210 is about £350 to £400 each. Second hand you could pick up a set for probably as little as £200 or £300 each. The price doesn't really depreciate much more than about fifty quid from the brand new price. They're a real investment in the sense that if you buy a set of decks for about £350/£400 each you're pretty much guaranteed you'll be able to sell them in four years' time for the same amount of money, give or take 50 quid. So they're a good investment in that way, they'll never lose their value because they are real work horses, you know they're just solid. It's not like buying a car and the day you buy it it loses a couple of grand. You are going to get pretty much what you paid for. If you buy anything less in terms of quality than a Technics – OK you've paid about £150 on a deck – the quality of the deck will be so bad that ultimately when you play out anywhere it's going to be on a Technics 1210 or it's going to be on maybe a Vestax, you know, the same calibre of deck.

So whatever you learn on, if you learn on a shit deck then when you go and play out, using something that's completely different, it will work and feel completely different and the adjustments will set you back a little bit. You'd be better off learning on the decks you'd be likely to use when you play in a club, I think. I would have difficulties using something lower than a Technics in terms of quality because they're just going to react differently. It's all about the stopping and starting of the record and it's about when you let go of the record how quickly it reaches its proper speed. When you slow it down it's how it reacts to the finer adjustments, when you're trying to beat match something. And if you got a shit deck you'll find that you'll do that and it'll just kind of go 'wwwuuuuh' and speed up again and then you'll just be there all day trying to get it right. And then you'll go to a club and play on Technics and what you've been used to doing and getting a certain kind of result from will just react completely differently and you'll be like oh, I'm back to square one. Why not just fuck all that man, and just learn on what you're going to be using.

PT: *Isn't that a lot of money to spend, though?*

AB: It's a lot of money, to go out and have to spend you know £300 or £400 on each deck, that's a hell of a lot of money, but like I said if you want to sell them in a year's time if you think,

"DJing's not for me," then you want to get what you paid for them. You buy shit decks for £150 and you try to resell them and you're going to get nothing. You're going to get like £40. Second-hand I bought – this is going back to when I was about 18 probably – going back say eight years, I bought two 1210s, a fairly good mixer, they were all flightcased you know like the kind of travelling boxes, and that was £600. For the whole thing which is not an unheard of deal. I could probably get them cheaper. I think the best thing with Technics is that you can buy them second hand because they don't fuck around.

PT: *How can you tell second-hand decks are still OK?*

AB: There are some tests you can make if you buy them second-hand. A good thing to do is, let's say you're buying a set of decks, take two records that are the same, put them on the decks and run them at the same speed to just listen and if they're perfectly in time with each other then you know that they're working properly. If one of them is slower then you're going to hear it. That's a really easy, obvious test. The other thing that's kind of silly is the little light with Technics. You press the little light and it pops up. Basically if it comes straight up and the light doesn't work then you can tell how old these decks are. That's something that'll go after three to four years. You can get these things changed – ultimately you can get decks serviced and with Technics nothing can go wrong with them that isn't serviceable. You never get to a point with them where someone says oh, it'll cost you too much to fix it, I'd get some new ones. They're not those kind of decks. So those are standard tests. Again the actual needle or cartridge on the deck you can swop around and change, no problem. You can adjust all the weights, so nothing can really happen to them that'll make them useless. Basically if you're serious about DJing you're going to want to get Technics anyway. The only thing I've never understood about them are the wires they have on them are really cheap, really basic wires. And if you're into it then the quality of sound is really important and if you think that they're industry standard in clubs then why put cheap wires on them, man? The cables probably cost about 3p.

PT: *What about mixers?*

AB: Mixers, you can't go wrong with them. I think my first mixer cost about £45 or something. Mixers are kind of irrelevant. If you're good with beat matching and knowing when to drop records then you can do that with any mixer. I have definitely DJed with the most basic mixer, ridiculous mixers. I DJed with mixers that didn't even have a headphone on them. Your mixer is really secondary. As long as it's got two volume channels on it and a monitor so you're hearing it before you play it then that's all you need. Buy a cheaper mixer and save your money. The technology with mixers moves much quicker. They are constantly changing, constantly getting better. The big difference is what kind of music you're playing. If you're playing hiphop and you're a scratch DJ then it's all about the crossfader – and it's going to be a crossfader that's, well depending on how you scratch, probably nice and short, really short between left and right, and smooth, probably a crossfader you can change. If you are a scratch DJ ultimately you're going to wear the little crossfader out and you want to just pop it out and swap it round, rather than buy a new mixer.

Maybe you want kill switches on it, maybe that's another way you want to scratch. If you're a house DJ then it's more a gradual thing when you mix so you should get one with dials on instead of faders because that's more how you mix. If you see a mixer with dials on then you'll think, oh that's more of a house

DJ mixer. If you're not a scratcher but you're more into blending sounds then get one with a lot of EQs on. If you're confident and you're up with the beat mixing and EQing then get one with all that and your ten second sampler. There's all these gadgets you can get for mixers but I think it's really secondary. Just go for a good brand name like a Numark or Vestax. But if you are on a level where you want to get a really good mixer, get an Allen and Heath – sound quality-wise they're great. They're brilliant. They've got these two filters on them which are incredible. You won't get tired of it. If you're into gadgets then get one with effects and shit on it. I'm not really down with those because a lot of the effects you get on a mixer are going to be quite simple and basic and really when you get to professional level you aren't going to be using those. It's more likely you'll get a little plug-in sampler loop thing. In terms of channels obviously you need a minimum of two channels to just run your decks through, but again if you're thinking maybe I want to add loads of effects down the line then think about that. As long as the crossfader can change because that'll be the first thing to go. You'll bring your left to right, it'll just leak and you'll still be hearing the other record. Get one where you can swop the crossfader.

PT: *What do you think about Vestax decks?*

AB: Vestax decks have made a real impact in the last couple of years, but because everyone's used to Technics it'll take them years to really get a lion's share of the market. Vestax decks technically do a little bit more. They have a wider pitch – Technics will be plus 8, Vestax could be plus 10 and beyond. They have a reverse switch on there, they have a quartz lock. They're really good. Sometimes they have a shorter arm on them as well which is better if you're a scratch DJ because obviously the physics would give the needle less space to move in. Because I'm used to Technics, if I'm trying to adjust the speed of a record I'm used to what the pitch will do if I move it just a millimetre. When you use a Vestax and do the same thing it's going to react differently. It'll take longer to beat match. It just slows you down a little bit but ultimately it's because I've been using Technics for years and Vestax I've used probably 10 times in my life. But if you learn on Vestax, no problem. On the Vestax you have buttons to speed it up and slow it down, whereas on a Technics you'd use your hand. Maybe it's the difference between driving an automatic and a manual car. You have loads of weird buttons – one that'll just bring you back to zero pitch. Which I find pointless, but even on the latest Technics Mark 3 they put that on. The only smart thing they did was they put a shield around the on and off switch. You know how with the on-off you just turn it, well if you're mixing and turning the platter then ultimately your hand will just knock it and turn it off. So they put a little shield around it so you can't do that. That's about the wisest thing they've done, but still the same shit wires, man!

PT: *How do you go about adjusting the weight of the tone arm?*

AB: Adjusting the weights can be complicated. You want to leave them as you found them, but let's say your record's skipping around a bit. If the arm is on the deck and it keeps moving around a bit then if you make the arm just a bit higher then it's obviously going to make it heavier on here, that's the physics of it to stop it skipping. If it's still bouncing around then on the back of the tone arm is the range dial. Bring it closer to that weight to make it heavier again. If it's too heavy and you can look at it and the needle is flat on your record then just adjust it the other way and it'll just bring it up a little bit. You also have an anti-skate thing which will stop it moving again from left to right. So if when the record's going round it's doing that a little bit then you can just lock that down. The other thing is inside the cartridge if you put a little weight in there that will make a big difference. Sometimes you see people and they put pennies on top of the decks – they always stick little 2ps or 1ps to the needle. You shouldn't do that but that's a way of getting round it. If you're in a bar and this thing is skipping round I'd get a penny and that'll be enough to weigh it down. Again that's why Vestax with the shorter arm can't do that, not that I really understand physics but I kind of understand the weight thing. If you're unsure then you can take Technics anywhere and get it serviced.

PT: *Where would you advise beginners to buy their equipment?*

AB: I would say go second-hand if you're on a budget, definitely. You're better off just buying one decent deck if that's all the cash you have to start with and just mix to the radio. If you've not got a big enough budget then you don't need to get two because you can mix to anything, you can mix to a cassette. I mean obviously you can only mix one way but in terms of practising you know, why not? Buy them second-hand, get a good cheap price, do a couple of checks on them so you're pretty sure they're OK. Check the pitches, move through the pitches at the same time and you'll see if they're the same speed. Buying second-hand can save you a lot of money. If you want to buy them brand new then pick up a copy of *DJ Magazine* or whatever else, the adverts are in the back but ultimately it's the same thing wherever you buy them. They're kind of standard. You get Technics 1210s, you get Technics 1200s, the only difference is the colour. There's no technical difference to them at all. 1200s are silver, 1210s are black. Mark 3s have the little zero pitch button and shield around the on-off switch, but again you don't need to worry about that either. The other thing of course is get slipmats for it as well. You need slipmats because when you're moving the records up and down with your hands they've got to slide freely and when you buy a deck they'll come with the rubber mat and lose those and just put the slip mats on. And then keep adjusting your needles. Ultimately keep replacing the needles once they feel worn out. Buying new needles is a hell of a lot cheaper than a new record collection. If you use a shit needle then you're just going to fuck all your records.

PT: *How can you tell if the needle's worn out?*

AB: If you've had a needle on there for a year I'd change it anyway. It'll cost you £20–£25 each. If you always have new needles on there then your records will always sound fresh and bright. Some DJs go to clubs and they always bring their own needles with them because they don't want to use shit needles on their records. I was DJing with Norman Jay on Saturday and he does that. You know he's got all these old classic records so he has his own brand new styluses. He'll go to a club and put them on so he knows that his records aren't getting fucked by someone's needles. The most annoying thing is if you play in bars. Bars have decks because that's what they want to have in there but the upkeep of them is really bad and that's when you want to bring your own styluses. Depends how precious you are about it.

PT: *At the bar my friend plays at you have to bring your own needles. They don't share needles.*

AB: DJs don't share needles! That's right! It's a good slogan, man. That's a T-shirt thing! OK, copywrited Ali B!

It came as a relief to know the girl had done good in getting Technics – to have the expert seal of approval, as it were. Incidentally, after attempting to play the grey import deck I managed to build through a shaver adaptor from Woolies, I gave up and took them back to the shop. What a relief it was when they happily exchanged them for ones with UK plugs. I made a big fuss and naturally insisted that the tiny red lead was already broken when I opened the box.

Being a hi-fi snob I liked the idea of having virgin decks untouched by the mucky fingertips of another DJ. Plus I felt reasonably reassured by the receipt and guarantee from the shop, even if the goods were probably made in Afghanistan. Being a credulous soul (has gullible *really* been taken out of the dictionary?) a rogue second-hand dealer would easily have sold me a pup. But buying used decks could have saved me some heartache three weeks later when I was made redundant by my 'new media' employers. Perhaps the non-work related internet surfing had been noted by *le* management after all.

2

Mixing

In my newly redundant state – otherwise known as 'freelancing' – unsurprisingly I had a lot more time on my hands. After the initial shock of my new media scrapheap situation wore off, I spent much of my time engaged in deep contemplation of my future.

It slowly began to dawn on me that growing up in the Eighties was potentially a major handicap to fulfilling my ambition of learning to DJ.

Perhaps in a time far, far away in the future when beards are in once more and the earth is run by Dave Lee Travis lookalikes as it was in the Victorian era, the Eighties may become fashionable again. If, of course, they were ever actually trendy at the time – I find it difficult to recall. Despite similar crimes against fashion and taste the Seventies have succeeded in achieving coolness again. However, as I write the possibility for a similar future for the Eighties looks bleak. There can be no argument that that anathema to clubbing known as School Disco has been a resounding success – now resident at trendy nightclub Pacha no less – however even School Disco has failed to make the Eighties passable. Love it or hate it – and many of us 20-somethings have fond memories of tripping the legwarmer fantastic to the likes of Spandau Ballet, Kim Wilde and Bananarama – the Eighties will never be cool.

The first Eighties obstacle to my turntabling success was the obvious fact that while photographs of me wearing big pointy earrings, a reversible jumper and Duran Duran sweatbands existed, I could never be cool like the guys featured in *Jockey Slut* and other such reading matter which now littered my bedroom. This self-knowledge was compounded by my well-documented shellsuit and New Kids On The Block period during the Nineties. True, I had burnt my precious posters of Danny Wahlberg (my girlhood crush ended very suddenly after witnessing Danny break into Bruce Willis' apartment in *The Sixth Sense* screaming blue murder and wearing nothing but a shocking pair of grey Y-fronts) but worse still was the lesser-known fact that as a precocious but prudish eight year old I had written to *Points Of View* to complain about Morrissey's pre-watershed appearance shirtless on *Top Of The Pops*. Beyond the pale were the Gazza videos hidden away for shame in my wardrobe at my parent's house. However the sins of youth are oft forgiven soon enough. Norman Cook – alias Fatboy Slim – has achieved the pinnacle of coolness despite early days of geekiness in The Housemartins and his more recent penchant for Hawaiian shirts.

The main technical problem was that Eighties DJs did not mix their records. So my idea of a DJ was in fact its not so distant but dinosaur cousin known as 'the disc jockey'. Disc jockeys looked like Tony Blackburn and sounded like Smashy and Nicey as they mumbled conceitedly on the microphone – more often than not all over the end of your favourite record. Usually they were called Darren, operated a mobile disco imaginatively called Darren's Discotheque which consisted of a makeshift cardboard box covered in strips of silver foil, and never had any of the records you'd request. If you'd asked them to beat-match they'd probably think you wanted them to go outside and fight your big brother.

Of course, DJ historians such as Bill Brewster will tell you that turntablists in the States such as Grandmaster Flash were mixing records right through the Eighties. But this insightful knowledge was mostly lost on the average Essex school kid *circa* 1986. The American craze of break dancing did break out occasionally in the Essex outskirts but most boys' mothers objected on the grounds that they'd squash their heads in spinning around on the floor – and from what I recall of primary school discos many of my potential suitors suffered from having rather flat heads already and could do with hanging on to the few brain cells God had given them anyhow.

Nowadays mixing is the first skill a DJ is expected to master, for you're not considered a fully fledged DJ unless you can seamlessly mix your tracks with the best of them. Unsurprisingly like everything else, it was something I was having a difficult time getting the hang of. I had thought nothing could top the trauma of putting my decks together but I was wrong. As I tried to drop one track in and get it in time with the other all I could succeed in doing was making noises reminiscent of a David Attenborough documentary I'd once seen about elephants stampeding. There I was playing 'Where's Your Head At' by Basement Jaxx on one turntable and trying to match up 'I Feel Love' by Depeche Mode on the other. It was hopeless. I couldn't get my head around it and my records were now all smeared with chocolatey finger marks. I tried counting the beats per minute (BPMs) to work out which records I could mix together until my brain was swimming. I decided it was time to call in the professionals and get some hands on mixing tuition.

Cosmo, alias Colleen Murphy, started DJing at the tender age of 14 in her native New York. Unlike others in her profession she learnt her craft mixing live on the radio, and played at the legendary Loft parties alongside icon David Manchuso. She has

33

DJed all over the world, playing regularly at Pacha and Fabric in London, and now has her own record label Bitches Brew with fellow DJ Nikki Lucas (see chapter 6) – so she was more than qualified to teach me some basic mixing techniques in the humble surrounds of my bedroom! First she showed me how to beat match a record. You do this by getting two records of a similar style and speed or BPM (beats per minute) – most house records are usually around 126 BPM – on the turntables and while the first record is playing you find the first beat of the second record and drop it in at the beginning of a bar in the first record, usually in what is known as a 'break' in the record – i.e. when there is a long instrumental part in which you can easily mix in another tune. You then have to work to get the two records in time with each other by moving the pitch control on the turntable up and down, depending on whether the second record is slower or faster than the record already playing.

This is easier than it sounds! It's tricky to work out which record is faster! You can also adjust the speed of the record by putting your finger lightly on the record label to slow it down or pushing it forward to speed it up slightly. All this is done in the headphones. When the two records are in time you carefully move the crossfader over so you can hear both records in the 'monitor' or speakers. Cosmo then showed me how to blend the sounds by using the EQs on the mixer, switching off the bass on the second record and then carefully turning the bass of the first record down as you gradually turn up the bass on the second record. Afterwards we sat and chatted about the finer points of mixing and her personal DJing philosophy.

PT: *What's the most important things to remember when mixing?*

C: First you need to pick two records that go well together. Then you need to match up the beats but then you need to know where to come in and when to get out of the mix. You need to have your hand on the pitch control at all times. If you're using a crossfader you can use that – the ratios – do you want more of record number one and less of record number two or half and half? Using the EQs – especially the bass or the kick drums – crossfading those, possibly crossfading the mids and the highs depending upon what's going on. Also making sure your gains are correct. They may not be the exact same setting on the board because records are pressed differently and the volumes coming across may be different. Those are the major things. Always listen to the monitor. You don't need to look at the record. Always have your hand on the pitch control while you're learning and just listen. Just use your ears – you'll hear what's going on.

PT: *How did you get into DJing?*

C: I started on the radio when I was 14 at my little high school, and then I went straight on at university and did radio there and commercial radio in Japan and started producing syndicated shows. While I was producing syndicated radio shows I was getting into dance music because I'd started going to The Loft and I'd heard this different kind of dance music than I'd ever heard in my life, and so that made me go out and buy the records. I was offered a radio show in New York on a non-commercial station. I took it and I was doing this kind of club mixing and from there I started to get into the lounges and the bars in New York and then the clubs and it just went on from there actually. So it started with radio for me, which it seems for a lot of other club DJs they do the opposite, they start off in the clubs and the bars and then they get onto the radio.

PT: *Did you always mix your records?*

C: I learnt to mix in front of people. It was really funny, I learnt to mix on a radio board which is very different from a DJing mixer because once something goes into programme you no longer have it isolated in cue in your headphones so you're mixing straight from the speakers and you're doing it live on air. It was incredible. I listen to the old tapes and it's like, Ooh! Doh! And I also learnt to mix in little lounges and bars, which is great because I didn't have Technics 1200s at home yet. So I kind of threw myself right into it and learnt to mix in front of people. I was a great programmer – I'd been programming music for ages, at least a decade by then – so that wasn't a problem as far as programming goes.

PT: *By programming you mean picking the records and putting them together?*

C: Yeah, what matches with what. How do you build a set, how do you bring it down, how do you start it, how do you end it. You can do that with any kind of music – rock music, anything. So I already knew that. It's something you have or you don't. But as for the technical side, no one taught me. I just kind of figured it out. And then when you watch people, how they do the EQs and things like that, you learn more as you go on. I'm still experimenting with stuff – now my whole thing is not cueing up a record but just mixing right as soon as I've put it on. I'm just challenging myself, and it's working, it's really wild! I just throw it in. I've seen other DJs like Derrick Carter do it – like, how do they do that?! Now I can do it. It's just experience – it's all experience and practice. I never practise at home, ever. I did when I was younger and I was making mix tapes at home and selling them. I wouldn't have time to make mix tapes now and I do everything in one take. I do radio shows for Japan and guest mixes for European and North American stations and I just do it in one mix or one take. I'm quite good at working under pressure – I just treat it as a live gig and my mixing skills are fairly good anyway.

PT: *They must be by now!*

C: I don't do fancy-fancy things like scratching but for house I'm really good at it but I don't practise and I think partly that's kind of helped me to be honest. I mean it's good to know some mixes that work . . .

PT: *So you'd have certain records that work together?*

C: Yeah, some people do. I don't always. But there's a couple of things that I know when I do it live, it really works and you'll end up doing it again some time. But I think practising makes you stick to certain formulas. I think it just makes you more nervous than you need to be. In the beginning you do need to practise a bit but it's just good to sit down and make some mix CDs. That's the best thing to do.

PT: *So then you can hear what it sounds like?*

C: Yeah, that's a great thing to do. I don't sit at home practising this mix and that mix – you just kind of feel it at the moment when you're playing. That's one of my philosophies – it's all about the moment. Because when you're DJing it depends on the crowd and all the different elements come into it and you have to really be with the moment because otherwise you can just stick a mix CD on. So you have to challenge yourself in that way. I'm doing a compilation album at the moment for Yellow, a French label, and it's not of the moment. I have to figure each thing out, each mix that's going to be on the CD, it's past and present, they can only licence a certain number of tracks because there's loads of things I want that I couldn't get, which means my whole original concept has changed. It's a completely different situation and I find it much more difficult because now I have to think it all out and I have to fix one of my turntables because it's broken! I had it all serviced with new cartridges and I found out there's one broken prong in the tone arm and I have to call an engineer today!

PT: *There's thousands of bedroom DJs out there practising for hours each day. Is this a good idea when you're starting out?*

C: It could be, yeah. I think everybody has their own methodology. If you're a hiphop DJ I can really see the point of that absolutely because there's a lot more technique involved. You really do have to know exactly where you put the needle on the record. It depends what style of music you're playing. If you're playing house, or trance or techno, it's just mixing. You probably do need to practise a bit when you're starting out. But really it's just knowing your records. Where is the break? When does it start to get boring? If it's just a track, can you mix it halfway through? How minimal is it? How much instrumentation is going on? I can remember things with records so easily. I catch melodies quickly, I catch bass lines quickly, I catch drums quickly. So I'm a musical person. If you're more musical you don't need as much practising really. For me rhythm comes very easily – it always has. Someone can sit me down with a drum kit and just give me a lesson and I can at least do some basic things on congas or whatever. I've always been able to do that. I play piano. With other people it takes a bit longer, that's not to say they can't be a great DJ but they might have to work harder at a number of things like that.

PT: *Do you think you could teach anyone to mix?*

C: I think you can try! But I think certain people just won't get it, whether it's the technological side or the rhythmic side. It's like certain people can sing on pitch, others are tone deaf. I may not know whether this is in the key of C or this is in the key of G and I may not know which exact key it is but I can hear it if the keys match or if it's dissonant – that's the word I'm looking for.

PT: *If it's jarring?*

C: Yeah. Sometimes dissonance works but usually in vocal stuff it doesn't. For things like that, knowing even sounds of kick-drums, kickdrum patterns, all these things come into play once you take it to different levels of mixing. Like certain drum sounds don't match other drum sounds and others go together so well that you can make it sound like one track. And I guess if you really get into it practising those things is good, practising your EQing.

PT: *So what are the basic techniques?*

C: First of all to me is programming, and even if you're not mixing but making it good. So that's the first thing, how do you set up a set? How do you start it, how do you bring it up and finish it? Are you going to finish on a high, on a low, or on a spacey thing? There's all different ways to do it. So programming is a first, then beat mixing, and then you get to the finer things like mixing in key, mixing in complementary keys or

EQing when you mix to make it sound smooth, so you don't have this doubled up kick drum or you don't have two vocals and the mids all the way up on both channels. Things like that. Generally when I'm doing the EQing I try to, if say turntable one has a lot of mid and has the bass rolled off, I'll bring up the bass on turntable two and roll off the mid to try to complement it. You don't want to overdo it on the bass or overdo it on the highs. So things like that you should always watch out for when you're mixing. You may hear a mix and the reason why it's not smooth is because they're not EQing it properly. They might have the BPMs matched perfectly and you hear all of a sudden the new record's come in, you can hear two kick drums now. Even if they're on time it's still two kick drums. Or you hear two people overlapping singing in different keys – that's the next level. And then after that it'll be using outside effects. Using the reverb, using echoes, loops.

PT: *You can buy mixers with effects on them, can't you?*

C: Absolutely. Most mixers nowadays have that on there. I have an old-fashioned mixer so I don't but I have a loop out where I could actually put effects units.

PT: *Do you tend to use them?*

C: It's the next thing I want to get into. A lot of people use that effect – 'shehshehshehsheshe sheh – shehshehshehshehshehsheh' (up and down) – thing that they always use now but it's a bit boring because everyone uses that same effect on the turntable. I've heard Francois Kervorkian use those outboard effects really well and creatively – almost in a dub type context. So that's my next area that I want to get into once my turntable's fixed!

PT: *How long have you been DJing now?*

C: Well if you count from the radio days, 20, if we count from clubs and using Technics 1200s, mixing and all that, it's about 12 years.

PT: *And you're still learning?*

C: Oh yeah. You find some people stop. I mean I hear DJs now I loved and listened to when I was going out to clubs and they still mix the same exact way and it's actually got worse – it's not as inspired anymore, so it depends. Some people get lazy and that's the thing, not to get lazy. With anything you do. It's the same with the records you're playing. I try to go to the shops once a week. You know, some people are still playing their promos, they're not going out to the shops to look for interesting things that they haven't been sent and all my favourite DJs still go to the shops. Danny Tenaglia still goes record shopping and he's one of the biggest DJs in the world and he's an interesting DJ. He's technically brilliant but he goes out and buys different things – he moves on musically. He's a phenomenal DJ and one of the reasons he is is because he hasn't gotten lazy. You have to support the industry too – the little record stores and labels that can't afford to mail you products.

PT: *It must be difficult for some DJs the older they get to keep up with it all.*

C: I agree. You look at some of these DJs out there and they're 50 or close to around 50 years old. Francois is 50, Tony Humphries is probably about the same, David Manchuso is in his late fifties. It is a tough lifestyle as far as if you're married and have kids or a partner or whatever, running around on planes all the time, it's exhausting. I think those people – the people in their fifties who are doing it – are famous and they can call a lot more shots. If they don't want to go somewhere and there isn't a first-class plane ticket they don't have to go!

PT: *What common mistakes do beginners make?*

C: I think they pay too much attention to the BPM – beats per minute – they're too focused upon beat mixing, and I did the same thing. As I said, I already had years of radio based programming so that wasn't a problem but sometimes the record's not meant to be mixed. And sometimes it's brilliant to bring a crowd right down and kick in with something new and different. You don't always have to mix every single record and you don't have to mix it a long time. Certain records go well for long mixing, other ones don't and you find new DJs are always trying to prove their mixing skills.

PT: *Everyone's obsessed with it, aren't they?*

C: They are. With every single record they're trying to prove their mixing skill and sometimes they shouldn't be mixing, they should leave it or other times there should be a short mix. So that's the biggest mistake and I still hear it even with good DJs. They're playing classics, things that are song orientated, and they'll cut it off before the good part comes because they want to show they can mix and there's no point, it's not about that. Hiphop is a very different thing, so this doesn't really pertain to that because it is about cutting quick and switching it up real quick, that's just how it always has been. It's about breaks, so that's a completely different thing. I'm talking about dance music – house, disco, techno, all that. So it's just getting obsessed with mixing every single record as long as you can. It's not necessary and a lot of times it sounds bad. Or people start mixing two vocals in two different keys. It's hard to mix two vocals if you're using the vocals at the same time. You usually have to do a call and response thing, so one will say one thing and the other will come back and reply. So it'll be the first two beats of the bar and the last two beats of the bar but you have to know how to do it.

PT: *Some people have told me you should have the BPM written on the record.*

C: Maybe but you can't always tell. I started mixing classics, which is more difficult than house because it's all live stuff mainly but of course the BPM changes throughout the record. I mean, some are really drastic and that's the thing with classics, you need to know where it changes – when the drummer speeds up – some drummers are steadier than others and then you can really see who's a good drummer as well! I pitch records sometimes while they're playing, sometimes it'll sound too fast or too slow to me, and I also like to move the BPMs throughout the night. Say all your records are 126 BPM – so you just play 126 all night? That would sound crap. Really music speeds up and slows down naturally anyway. Anyone who plays any music knows that.

We're used to playing a wide range of music. Reggae is about 80 and some of the Hi-NRG disco – especially the gay kind – is in the 130s. So there's a whole spectrum. So you do need to know what goes together. I can pretty much listen to something now and tell you what BPM it is because of all the classics I used to play. They have BPM monitors on mixers but they don't work very well and it's better to ignore them, although it may be useful when you're learning. There isn't a huge difference between 126 and 128 because that's why you have a pitch control, there is a big difference between 116 and 130 because if you start pitching it's gonna sound wack. Some techno sounds great pitched down as long as there's no vocal in it. Once you get vocals you have to watch what you're pitching or it'll sound like Mickey Mouse – although it's OK if you're a garage DJ! I guess everyone has their own technique!

PT: *How is it different mixing in your bedroom to mixing out at a venue when maybe the equipment doesn't work or you're not familiar with it?*

C: Equipment is one thing. Usually every time you go some place there's something wrong.

PT: *What? Even at your level?*

C: Almost always. The clubs in Italy have sound engineers on site and Fabric is great too, they have sound engineers walking around, room to room. Everything's sound checked before you get there. So real professional clubs usually don't have problems but that's a minority. Most places are not like that – there's always something and just obvious stuff you would never consider doing as a setup. People in most bars, even certain clubs, look at the music as secondary, they're more concerned with the decor. So they'll have a monitor on the floor, which is the stupidest place for a monitor – ideally it should be in front of you and up. On the floor it's reverbing and you have to lean down to mix.

I did this music lounge in the West End and this place is billing itself as a music lounge. Every night they had DJs and good DJs too. We did a night there and one of the turntables wasn't even playing on both channels, in stereo. This is every week – "Can you fix this?" – it would cost £200, they charge

£9 for drinks. So they wouldn't. It was "Oh yeah, yeah, yeah, we will next week." So it finally got to the point where I thought, I'm gonna screw these people up. I just played on one turntable all night and I just took the record and put the record on and played it. When it came off I took the record off very slowly, put it back in its jacket, then looked for another record, then put it on the turntable. They were so embarrassed. I said to the people there, well obviously they don't have enough money to fix the turntable. The manager was sending me bottles of champagne and I quit that night. Now that's what I do to prove a point. The music isn't secondary. They changed the decor three times while I was there – so the wallpaper was more important.

PT: *Wow!*

C: So you need to be more adaptable. You need to know about the sound system. Nothing should be distorting – you shouldn't have red lights on your mixer. What a lot of places do is turn the amp right down because they don't want it blown and turn the mixer right up but the signal from the mixer gets distorted and then it amplifies. So I turn the amp up and turn the mixer down. This is schoolgirl stuff but a lot of DJs don't know it and you get there and the gain is all the way up and the system's blown out.

The other difference from bedroom mixing is there's people and you have to deal with them! Certain DJs just play for crowds, then you have people who play the trendy stuff in bars but they're still all manipulating the crowd, then you have people like me who might play a few things people will know but also a lot of stuff they won't know. I like to expose people to different types of music – so that's my challenge to keep them there but take them to different places. You have to deal with the space – are you going to play hard core techno in a tiny room? Probably not! Ballads in a room that holds 2,000?

Probably not! It even comes down to lighting. Brighter clubs – it's more of a happy vibe – then in dark clubs you can do deep techno. You probably wouldn't have a really bright drum 'n' bass club. The kind of people there. All of these things count and that's what makes a great DJ because some people are great bedroom DJs but you can't put them in front of a crowd. They might have a programme that they want to come and do but it's not about that. It's about really being with the moment and adaptable with your equipment.

PT: *What about all these different musical terms like deep house? What do they mean and how can you avoid turning up to a gig with the wrong type of music?*

C: Promoters generally don't know what they're talking about when it comes to music, to be completely honest. The only ones who do are ones who DJ themselves. You learn early on – don't listen to the promoters.

PT: *Do your own research?*

C: Yes. If it's someone's own night and they DJ there then that's a whole different thing but if it's a promoter, don't listen. There's certain terms – 'underground'. What is underground? Everyone thinks what they do is underground. So a garage DJ thinks he's underground, a deep house DJ thinks he's underground because it's not commercial. Then a techno DJ thinks he's underground. It's just the stupidest term anyway. House can mean different things. To some people house is really vocally and happy, to other people it's very dark or very tracky. What's deep house? I don't know! Garage is different in the States to what it is here. It's vocal house in the States and here it's what was called two step for a while, which kind of goes into

46

R&B as well. Then there's progressive. I guess everything else is not! I think some people who make music make it to fit into a certain genre and it's not always the most inspired music.

PT: *Have you had any horror stories?*

C: Oh the worst! Here's another example of a promoter not knowing anything about music. I was doing this lounge night in New York – light house, disco and funk – but this Swedish manager, he doesn't like hiphop and he think it attracts the wrong element, so no hiphop, no hiphop, no hiphop – that's the mantra. I show up one day and realise the venue is closed for a private party. No one told me this but I'm still the DJ. It was for the New York Knicks – a basketball team and I had no hiphop! I really wanted to pick up that Swedish guy and strangle him. I was getting so much hassle – the DJ booth is raised up and these guys are looking me right in the eye. But finally I had some old funk and I was able to save the day – but they're not going to listen to house, that's gay people music. That's the way black or white basketball people in New York think! Vocal house is for gay guys! It's funk and hiphop, R&B – that's it. That was the worst experience and the manager was nowhere to be seen that night! So from then on I always had hiphop with me.

PT: *I suppose as the DJ you're a bit of a target.*

C: It's like when someone waits tables and the kitchen fucks up. Do they go yell at the chef? No, they yell at the waitress. Don't shoot the DJ!

I was surprisingly pleased with myself after Cosmo's visit. She was really patient but it wasn't exactly easy learning to beat match in front of one of my heroes – a successful female DJ. For a start, the record kept slipping out of my fingers because my hands were sweating nervously. But somehow I'd managed to pull it off – beat match the records I was using, which were 'I Feel Love' by Depeche Mode – one of my fave records – and the B-side to 'To Get Down' by Timo Maas, and successfully EQ them. In fact, praise indeed from Caesar, Cosmo said that the two records I'd randomly picked out because I only had about 10 house records went really well together and she'd mix them together if she had them in a club. I was well chuffed! The question was, with Cosmo gone and left to my own devices could I sustain this level of mixing magic?

3

Scratching

I was beginning to come to terms with the fact that learning to DJ wasn't as easy as it looked. I'd thought it was just a matter of getting tooled up with the right decks, buying some records and then you were well away but it was clear there was more to it than that. Mixing was tricky and I wasn't at all convinced I'd got the hang of it, despite Cosmo's expert tuition and endless patience with my clumsy attempts. Miraculously I'd managed to pull it off while she was on hand to give me guidance but alone in my flat I found it difficult to recreate the successful mix every time and the elephant noises would recur.

I gathered some of my favourite tunes together – 'You Got The Love' by Candi Staton, which always just sends my spine tingling like nobody's business, 'Lazy' by Xpress 2 – it doesn't matter how many millions of times you've heard this one but it still sounds fantastic, David Byrne's vocals are just spot on and when the first few notes kick in it's just magic – and the ringbang remix of 'Electric Avenue' by Eddie Grant. Sometimes I could get the mixes just right but mostly it was all over the shop. The Eddie Grant remix had these weird African drums in the intro and although they sounded amazing it was difficult to get them to blend in with anything much.

I longed to mix those really classy James Bond theme songs like 'Diamonds Are Forever' by Shirley Bassey in with my house tunes to do something different but the BPMs were all over the place and while I still couldn't manage the basics I was hardly going to run before I could crawl. Sometimes I felt so frustrated I wanted to chuck my headphones across the room but then I remembered how much they cost and restrained myself.

I'd always kidded myself that I was reasonably musical so the struggle came as a bit of a shock. I'd sung in the choir at school – albeit not very well – and played the flute briefly in the school orchestra (I refer you to the previous disclaimer) admittedly before my long-suffering teacher Mr. Thomas finally gave up on me. I thought this would be sufficient qualification. After all, most of the hooded young lads I saw hanging around the vinyl in HMV – sporting jeans with the crotch down to their knees – didn't look like they'd recognise one end of a wind instrument from the other – apart from maybe their own. It was clear I needed to put in some serious practice if I was going to perfect the technique.

"How do you get to Carnaby Hall?" asked one of my mates, who shall remain nameless. "I don't know," I said. "Maybe you can find it on Streetmap.co.uk if you know the road it's on."

"Practise, practise, practise!" he exclaimed triumphantly. I looked at him and shook my head. "Er, I think you'll find it's *Carnegie* Hall in New York," I replied, gently. "You're thinking of Carnaby Street in London, mate," but I took the hint all the same. It was time to knuckle down to some serious mixing homework. Suddenly it dawned on me the advantage these baggytrousered youths had over me – fanaticism. They didn't think twice about sitting mastering a Playstation game for 18 hours a day and could easily apply the same dedication to learning to DJ, which would benefit them whether they could recognise a treble clef or not.

As a family we were all wannabe musicians. Years ago my Dad had been in a band and still fancied himself as a rock'n'roller. He had a raucously loud Tom Jones style soul voice that was now reserved for use in the shower. One of the lingering memories of my teenage years was of him regularly standing outside my bedroom door with a cup of tea singing 'Hi Ho Silver Lining' at the top of his voice, drowning out Jason Donovan or other such horrors that would have been playing on my stereo at the time. Dad's love of music had sadly not led to stardom – more's the pity for all of us – but he had worked for a while as a record rep in the Seventies for Phonogram and along with my Mum – a massive Elvis and Bob Dylan fan – had built up a respectable vinyl collection. As a sixth-former of 17, once my music tastes had matured a little and I had put my childish ways – namely Donovan and Minogue – behind me, I used to sneak out my parents' Beatles records and play them on the record player when they were out. Vinyl was a thing of beauty to me even then, accustomed as I was to ugly cassette tapes.

Sadly these records now languished unheard on a shelf in the living room at my parents' house as the record player, which dated from the Sixties, had finally given up the ghost . Not that my parents had played any of them for years anyway – apart from the odd regrettable burst of Barry Manilow to indulge my mother. One morning when I was down at my parents' in Romford for the weekend I eyed them greedily as I attacked my fried egg.

"Don't suppose I could have some of those records for my collection, could I?" I asked, assuming the answer would be yes. "I'd really like that *This Is Soul* album you've got, mum."

My parents blinked back at me across the breakfast table and clutched at each other's hands, uttering a horrified gasp. "You're not going to be doing that *scratching* thing with them, will you?" my mum demanded, pronouncing the word with distaste as though it were some sordid pastime.

Scratching. I hadn't even given it a thought but it was something as a DJ I certainly needed to learn. The next step as it were. "Not right now, but I will be learning to, although I won't be scratching your records of course." My mother stood protectively in front of the shelf.

"I don't think we'll be letting you have them," she said slowly. "They might not be worth much but they have a lot of sentimental value and we've spent years building up this collection."

I quickly realised with a gulp of shame how in my greed I'd misjudged the situation and I felt just how difficult I'd find it to part with any of my tiny collection of vinyl – even the second-hand ones I'd bought that were horribly warped beyond recognition.

"I'm sorry," I said. "Just forget I mentioned the idea." I knew I could pick most of them up for about a quid in a second-hand shop anyway and I felt guilty, as though I'd suggested desecrating some kind of musical shrine. My parents still looked vaguely uneasy.

"You can have that old Ravi Shankar album if you want," my Dad suggested uncertainly.

My thoughts turned to scratching. Maybe I was jumping the gun a bit when I hadn't even mastered the rudiments of mixing but I had to try it out. Back in my room at home I listened to some of my Jurassic Five records to try to get an idea and managed to make some scratching–type noises with an old knackered Blak Twang record I couldn't play but I didn't feel I was really getting to grips with it. It was time once again to call in the professionals.

Cutmaster Swift is a scratching legend. A world-class performer, winner of the famous DMC world championships and pioneer of many scratching techniques, he now comperes the tournament and teaches the craft at the DMC UK headquarters as well as still DJing and making 'battle' scratching records. I was not worthy even to touch this guy's slipmat but he was still happy enough to fill me in on the strange world of turntablism and teach me a few basic techniques along the way.

PT: *Where does scratching come from?*

CS: Scratching came from cueing. Grand Wizard Theodore discovered it. He didn't want to lose part of a record when his mum was talking to him and he was moving the record backwards and forwards while she was chatting and he thought, wow this sounds really good! Then he started just messing with it and so scratching was born.

PT: *How does it complement the mixing?*

CS: Scratching is the DJ's vocal over an instrumental. One has to take precedence. Either the vocal is the main feature or the scratching is – you can't have them both. When we scratch words we tend to make them stutter – we want it to sound as naturally human as possible, so if I'm scratching the word "go" I'll say, "Ggggoo ge go go," and I could do it to the rhythm of 'Mary Had A Little Lamb'. In some bands the turntable is recognised as an instrument and they've got their DJs doing solo parts. There's thousands of techniques and they're still being created now. I'd be a liar if I said I knew them all because I'd have to know every DJ on the planet. A lot of people say scratching is the most difficult thing in turntablism to do because although you're only using one turntable and one mixer it's the rhythms.

PT: *How do you hold the record?*

CS: A lot of beginners are nervous about how to hold the

record. It's important that you try to be very comfortable. There is a certain width restriction between the mixer and the turntable. You want to position yourself in a way that you're not going to hit the arm. On the traditional club turntable position you have half the record to scratch. Then it's a case of cueing the record backwards and forwards. Very little movement is applied to the crossfader because all it is is a switch. It's on or it's off. Again with the record it's either forwards or it's back. Hold the record and get comfortable with releasing that record and cueing it. When I start the record I want it to sound as if it's starting proper. I don't want it to slur or start halfway in the record. I'm looking at this label – where it says promo – and using that as a reference point. You could have a go right now and see how good I am!

PT: *Yikes! Alright!*

CS: You're not applying too much pressure to the turntable which is great. When you apply too much the plates under the turntable will start moving all over the place. Just be very light and let it go. You've got to be consistent in where you let it go. Now the very first scratch is a rub. Which is this *[he moves the record up and down to make a 'whuh' sound]*. Now you try! You've got to keep it to a rhythm – one, two, three, four – consistently. Now we're going to try and do it with the fader. Open the fader, release the record, close the fader and pull back the record. This is called cutting.

PT: *This isn't as easy as it looks!*

CS: It's a bit like rubbing your stomach and patting your head.

PT: *Or learning to drive!*

CS: This is a new record and it's a bit slippery. What we tend to do is wear the lacquer out so it doesn't slip so easily in our hands. So when you see a DJ who scratches a lot you'll see a lot of fingerprints on his records! Which does do the record some kind of damage – it gets worn out. So those are the basic techniques and you can mix them together. *[He does a sequence of rubbing and cutting.]* Again you should have heard the pattern I was doing there – that's the way it works. You've also got chirps – it gives you a different effect. DJ Cash Money used the technique and called it babuggamas because it sounded like that. But Jazzy Jeff and the Fresh Prince did this record called the 'The Magnificent Jazzy Jeff' and the Fresh Prince says, "My DJ is so great he can make the record sound like a bird," and it really did by using this technique so that's how it got the name.

Then you've got transforming. What I'm doing is chopping the sound up. This is the word 'fresh' and I'm going to chop some parts of it up – 'freh heh-heh-heh-esh'. I can chop it forwards or backwards and again I try to make it into a pattern and think of a rhythm in my head.

The curve on this mixer isn't great – it's important to have a good curve. Because it's a club orientated mixer it's got a fade point on it where you fade one turntable into the other. Whereas this other mixer over here doesn't have that on it. It's straight open and really sharp, which is important when we do various scratches.

Then there's crabs. Crabs is when you roll your fingers and you're brushing against the fader – do you hear that stuttering kind of sound *[the fingers move like a crab from side to side when he brushes them against the fader]* – so you're chopping up the sound a lot faster. You can hear all the different sounds you're getting out of the one sound.

The needle scratches are like a flaring, another technique. Flaring is like what we're doing now because before when we used the fader we had it shut and then open so you hear it, and it's a case of chopping it in quick so you hear the cutting in, but with flairing the whole fader is in reverse. So the fader's mainly open and now we're chopping out the part. Before we were opening the sound so you can hear it – we're now closing the sound for the parts we don't want you to hear, which creates a virtual scratch. The scratch is going twice as fast. Now we can put the techniques together and that's basically how it works. Usually we have the turntables turned the other way, giving you three quarters of the record to play with. That's what we call battle mode and it's the standard.

PT: *Your fingers move so fast!*

CS: Well this mixer isn't really appropriate for what we're doing. We often use ones that are more simple and the faders are smoother. It's only over the last eight to ten years that the equipment has started to catch up with what we were doing. Now we're getting a lot more efficient because we're not being held back by the equipment. Something I tell our students is get familiar with the mixer. I see so many DJs in clubs when the warm-up DJ is playing and they're just happy to get on the equipment and play. "I'm the star of the show, it's my turn to go and do this show," and they don't study the equipment. When you're using stuff in a club that's not your own there could be all types of problems, like the headphones don't work properly, the functions on the mixers. So I always try to break the ice with any DJ that's playing – say how's it going, what's the equipment like, get an inside view because if he says it's alright and he's doing a good job then it makes me feel better and gives me more confidence to do the job. Sometimes you get these DJs and they come in with their boxes and they're like, "I'm on in the next five minutes, you've got to hurry up." It happens although we try to be professional about it. There are incidents when DJs in clubs will be mean to other DJs and bend the needles and stuff like that because they're competition. If they do badly you look better!

PT: *Have the techniques changed much?*

CS: At the time I was coming out DJing was quite different to the way it is now.

Through people like DJ Cash Money it changed to the third generation of techniques and it became more creative. The turntable was now being used to create its own compositions rather than just change slightly parts and licks of records. Although the pioneer Grandmaster Flash was doing that when he was keeping the beat and the instrumental part of a record looping for endless amounts of time and changing it into a new composition, what turntablists were doing was chopping those sounds and rearranging them in a real time manner no different to how a bass player picks up a guitar and plays the normal key ranges of notes you know, but it's his own riff and that's what turntablists are doing. There were standard techniques and there were experimental ones. A lot of things I did people didn't understand. There's lots of my techniques that are now incorporated into turntablism today and people have changed the names. But I've got video proof of all the things I've created.

PT: *What do you teach a complete beginner?*

CS: I do courses here at DMC and the first thing I try to instil in anyone is have your own identity. I see mixing as like telling a story. You've got to have a start, a highlight and a brilliant ending, and that's something anyone can understand. You don't have to be technical. Don't feel frightened to experiment and there's no rules. Try and communicate things in your head because we all hear things in a different way. Timing is a very vital point so we try to establish faults and improvements.

The first thing with scratching is that it involves a pattern. You've got to have a rhythm or melody in your head. For example we take 'Mary Had A Little Lamb' and do it in a scratch form called a 'rub'. You rub the record as I showed you 'chuh, chuh, chuh, chuh' and I'll show them that same pattern using different techniques. As soon as they can start acknowledging the techniques within that pattern, because they all add a different feel to it, then that's when you start understanding the most important aspect of scratching. It's not just being able to do technique, after technique, after technique – it's having a rhythm in your head and being able to execute it as accurately as possible.

Beat juggling is a bit harder because that involves moving from left turntable to right turntable consistently and keeping it all in time. It involves a lot of coordination. We go right back to the basics of what Grandmaster Flash did. Timing – just keeping the record running from one turntable to the other and then slowly increasing that speed and keeping it in time. We want to try and make the record look as visually pleasing as possible. When moving at certain speeds you'll only hear a record a certain way when it's riding forwards and playing backwards. So we actually put markers on the records – I don't know who pioneered the idea of marking a record up but it seems to be something basic. You think, how do I know where I'm cueing this record from? For example this word 'Battle One' on the record I have here is pointing at you, so if we say this is six o'clock you could count round one, two, three, four, etc. So I know when I wind it back to there that's always going to be one because of the way the label is set. That will be my cue point. I teach the students to count the number of rotations. You know if it's rotated once you've got to rotate it back once for it to go back to one. That's beat juggling. Cueing these various points you can rearrange that count and through timing it will actually sound fluent. Once they've marked up their records we get them used to looking at a certain point on the record and knowing confidently that that's where that record's going to say one. Then they can start being more adventurous and changing the timing. Turntablism is all about time signatures, it's about pitch, creating music and it's very important that the audience can feel a consistent tempo because if not, and you're asking them to clap, the clapping could be all over the place!

PT: *Are all the people who take your courses experienced DJs?*

CS: I've had people who had no knowledge of mixing but I always say the most important thing is knowing your music. You've got to study the way music's arranged and built – from the intro, verse chorus and maybe an instrumental section. Then it's a case of taking one bit out and putting another bit in.

PT: *Did you teach yourself?*

CS: Yes, because at that time there weren't any videos to learn from, there were some movies and documentaries but you saw, you heard and you tried to interpret to the best of your ability. There were no courses. With turntablism it's a prestige thing to say you're self-taught but in all honesty we do learn from every-one else – the people who inspire us. It's just that with teaching yourself you're taking a longer route to learning because there's no one to say you're doing it wrong.

PT: *Would you call yourself a bedroom DJ then?!*

CS: I'm definitely a traditional bedroom DJ! I had a passion for music from birth because my Dad had his own sound system. He was into music a lot so it was passed on. I found a calling with hiphop music in particular because it was something new and exciting and it took mixing into an aspect which was totally alien but I understood it naturally. Like most bedroom DJs you get some money and some equipment together, starting obviously with the equipment that's not around today much – just very basic turntables, learning the aspects of timing really more than beat mixing. The turntables I had at the time didn't have pitch control. I'm not sure I was aware of those functions because I'd never actually seen a proper professional setup.

PT: *How old were you?*

CS: I was about 14 and before I got some decks I was using my mum's hi-fi and I used to just pause button the mixes, so her pause button was probably broken by the time I'd finished with it! But I used to loop the record, by pause buttoning it – trying to just extend certain parts of it, just getting the whole idea of timing and bars. Then I managed to get two disco turntables, mobile ones, again they didn't have any pitch control, they were belt driven and that taught me the difference between self-driven turntables and direct driven tables. A belt driven turntable would never start up as accurately as a direct driven and they would wobble. It was a very frustrating period in my time of DJing. Because at the time it was all new I was fortunate enough to meet other people who also had the same passions and probably knew a bit more or a little less. So it was a case of meeting up with them and talking about something and realising, wait a minute, so that's how that's done! We were all teaching each other.

PT: *How did you turn professional?*

CS: When I started out there was no focus. Nowadays things are more directional. If you want to be a club DJ it starts off with demo tapes, CDs, going to clubs where people you like play and being influenced by them and trying to get into their market. Everything's got a field now. When I started out it was like, yeah I like music, I like DJing – let me do it for the sake of doing it. There wasn't a championship to win.

I got my first taste of what a semi-professional DJing situation was through a guy called the Imperial Mixer. He was one of the first DJs I saw with Technics 1200s. The first time I saw them was on the 'Buffalo Girls' video by Malcolm McClaren and I heard these turntables were about £200 each and I said, "£200 for a turntable, you must be crazy!" I wasn't as fortunate as these kids today with Xbox and Playstation! We formed a crew called the Imperial Mixers. I was probably a leech then because I didn't have any equipment but I had a passion and I would say that's most important. So that when you get on the turntables you don't want to get off and you're so eager to learn you pick up as much as possible in the little time you've got.

Through the Imperial Mixers we formed one of the first DJ groups. There were lots of DJ groups growing up at that time but now it seems to be the fashion or a standard. We did a lot of support for the early acts like Curtis Blow, a very early Run DMC – bands that were coming over from the States and again we were seeing how they were doing it. The Americans were the initial pioneers of hiphop. At that time I was still bedroom – I didn't tell my parents much about it and as long as I wasn't bringing no police home they were happy! From that it was a case of going into nightclubs and running up and down the country. I got certain exposure through Tim Westwood when he was on the pirate radio stations and a club he was putting on called Spatz, which catered for a lot of street DJs, break dancers, rappers.

I didn't get into the professional aspect until about '87 when I first heard about Chad Jackson winning the DMC Championships. I thought it wasn't really for me – I thought, well I'm a bedroom DJ and to get to that kind of stage you've got to know people and I thought my stuff would have been a bit too raw.

PT: *What changed your mind?*

CS: In '88 a partner of mine DJ Pogo said he was going to enter the DMC competition. I thought, if it goes well for him I might enter next year. He won one of the heats and I met up with him at this club and he said, yeah they've got some great prizes – they're giving out these jackets. And when I saw this jacket – nice leather jacket with Technics UK Heat Winner on the back and I was like, Jesus that jacket is wicked! Seriously, I entered this competition just to win one of them jackets! I mean, Technics was a high status item to have. If you wanted to be taken seriously you had to have Technics decks. I had some cheap decks and obviously I didn't tell people what they were.

I entered the competition and fortunately I won one of the heats and suddenly I'm a winner and I'm in the competition that's going to go to the final. It's really happening. I still didn't tell my parents about it. I'd won underground competitions before but nothing serious. I realised that this was a whole different ball game. I would practise for hours without any real focus – but now I was practising for the UK final. Now I'll be officially saying I'm the best DJ in the UK.

When it came to the night of the final I was fortunate enough to win it. DJ Pogo went on last – and they usually saved the best DJ till last – but unluckily he got stylus problems. Then I was thrown into a totally different realm. I was at the light at the end of the tunnel but now there was a totally different tunnel to go through because I was in the World Final in 1988. DJ Cash Money was someone who inspired me greatly and I found out he was representing the US. I couldn't believe it. I met him at the convention when they all came over and I was like, come over to my house for a scratch. I wasn't really worried about the competition anymore! I lost my focus. I learnt a valuable lesson from Cash that it's business first, pleasure afterwards and he went on to win it that year. The next year I felt I had a responsibility to the UK to win it in 1989. No matter what, I'm winning that world title!

PT: *How did you work out your routine?*

CS: I tried to convey the technical aspect of turntablism as it's called now – at the time it was known as battle DJs – and I also had a very entertaining visual side. One of the reasons I didn't think DMC was right for me was that I was very technical but not everybody can understand technical brilliance. It's something people sing praises about after it's all gone because they've absorbed it by then. So I tried to encompass a routine that you could appreciate visually as well as audibly and technically and actually this is where my mum came in! I showed her the routine and she was like, yeah it looks great! She was telling me what to wear now!

PT: *How did winning the world championship change you?*

CS: I'd been to Amsterdam and little places like that but I'd never travelled the world extensively as I did when I won the UK finals. I was going to places like Spain and Italy. I'd never been very good at geography at school – I was like, why learn another language, I'm not going to go there, am I?! And there I was going to all these places!

After a few hours in Cutmaster Swift's studio I couldn't wait to get home and experiment on the turntables with some of the techniques I'd learnt, although I realised I was a long way off securing a title like 'Grand Master or Mistress'. Maybe Grand Plonker might be more appropriate or Pipemeister as Nina my flatmate insisted on calling me.

The other thing which was apparent after my failed parental record stealing mission was that I needed to do some serious record shopping because with only a handful of dance records and other pieces of vinyl dating from the Seventies I could hardly call myself a DJ. My credit card began to sweat with anticipation. After all there was still the £1,000 worth of DJing equipment on it that hadn't been paid off and now I'd lost my job and was 'freelancing' as a journalist life was all a bit hand to mouth. I would wake up in the middle of the night in a cold sweat worrying about how I was going to pay the rent as none of the magazines I'd written for had felt like coughing up my cheques yet. My mum kept nagging at me to sell my precious decks. NEVER! I swore, on the sleeve of my beloved Curtis Mayfield *Superfly* album.

4

Packing Vinyl: How To Buy Records

It was obvious that the finer technical elements of DJing such as mixing and scratching hardly came easily to me despite the top quality teaching I was lucky enough to receive from Cutmaster Swift at DMC no less. I feared I was attempting to make Fatboy Slim from Alan Partridge's ear. Frankly, as I'd said to Cutmaster, it was all too reminiscent of my two years spent trying to learn to drive. Tears, £2,000 and countless appalling parallel parks later I'd managed to fool some credulous examiner into thinking I knew what I was doing and somehow scraped a pass but had never darkened a driving seat since. I hoped the same wouldn't be true for my DJing. I had no wish to develop turntable fright at this early stage in my fledgling career.

At least shopping for records sounded straightforward enough. After all, retail therapy is something we females of the species excel at in comparison with our male counterparts who tend to lag several yards behind us moping miserably on any shopping expedition, whether the venue be the clothes boutiques of Covent Garden or the catfood aisles of Tesco's. However, to excuse the pun, with record shopping the tables were often turned and it was the girlfriends left yawning in a corner. My evil ex had spent a great deal of our 11-month long relationship dragging me around the trendy second-hand record shops of Berwick Street in London's Soho.

During these trips my energies were heavily concentrated on trying not to look bored out of my tiny mind while the ex stood in the listening booth checking out the 55 or more records he'd picked up, invariably trying very hard to look cool in his polo neck jumper and Levis twisted jeans with the bottom cleavage spilling over – no easy task for any man. Now the shoe was on the other foot and I was the one scouring these record shops, the problem I found was that often the places were littered with clones of my ex so it was difficult to find the record you were looking for in amongst the myriad Firetrap shirts and trendy Vans trainers. More than anything else I dreaded bumping into him with a bag full of vinyl. I could almost hear him now: "What do you think you're doing with those records? You don't *seriously* think girls can DJ do you?!"

Vinyl shops can be intimidating. There are few women around and you have to look like you are a seasoned DJ and with the vibe, man. First you have to contend with the serious looking guys showing off their 'underground' record bags while they slowly thumbed through the latest releases and hope they didn't twig you'd never heard of any of the artists on the vinyl sleeves you were carefully studying. Then there were the record shop assistants, 99 per cent of whom were twenty-something males covered in metal piercings and most of them reminded me of the little know-it-all geeks in *High Fidelity*. It was no good going up to the counter and asking for the latest Britney Spears album, you would be laughed off the premises.

I was too scared to go up to them and ask them what I should be buying so I just picked up random stuff that looked interesting, bought it and played it at home. Hypothetically you were supposed to be able to listen to the records in the store but it could be difficult trying to get access to the listening booths, occupied as they were by gangly 12-year-old youths in bandannas. It was clear that I needed to find my own personal vinyl shopper.

Adam Dewhurst is one busy man. Not only does he own and run highly successful DJ magazine *Jockey Slut* and lifestyle title *Sleaze Nation* but he also finds the time to combine his career as a publishing magnate with DJing under the moniker Daddy Ad. Fitting me into his busy schedule he gave me some handy tips on buying records and explained how girlfriend DJ Cosmo (see chapter 2) has taught him to take better care of his vinyl collection.

PT: *At what age did you start buying records seriously?*

AD: Probably about 12 or 13 but I was always surrounded by music.

PT: *Roughly how many records do you own now and what kind of music?*

AD: No idea how many but classics, reggae, disco, house, rock, blues, jazz and everything in between.

PT: *How many records do you buy a week?*

AD: Only a handful. I'll only buy a record if it's really really good, but unfortunately there is a lot of crap out there. Filtering through it's tough sometimes. Most of my records get sent to me though.

PT: *Was it intimidating going into record shops at first or did you find it easy? Were the assistants helpful or were they a bit snooty?!*

AD: Scary business. My girlfriend used to work in record shops from an early age and I would have loved to have found a shop she worked in (except she was in New York). When I first started going shopping it was daunting. They did seem snooty and still are in some cases. But most people who work in record shops have got to be good people if they like music that much (it doesn't pay a fortune, long hours, lots of translating la de da renditions of something probably sampled a thousand times and you need to know your shit – it must be a bit like DJ requests sometimes). It's weird though, one day you just seem to know everybody and finding that last copy is a lot easier.

PT: *How do you decide what you want to buy?*

AD: I generally either get sent it, hear it in the office, hear my girlfriend play it and sometimes hear somebody I'm playing with play it. We usually get them way before radio.

PT: *Where do you shop?*

AD: Generally the same haunts in London but I love going to old collectors' shops in provincial towns. It's not unusual to find a pile of your must have classic records of all time for a few quid. You've got to love a bargain.

PT: *What do you do when you enter a record store?*

AD: Say hi to the manager and see if there is anything great they've heard (this is not recommended if you do not know the manager). Have a flick through the new releases, see whose names, labels, etc., I recognise or I've been looking for. Have a listen, make a decision. With old collectors' shops there have been some great discoveries through lucky dip.

PT: *What's the best way to get hold of the best records? Do you need to have a good relationship with the people running the record shops?*

AD: Yes but it's all about knowing the producers, labels and distributors too. There is so much stuff out there and some doesn't even get released. The market is clogged with crap and majors.

PT: *Are you a member of a record pool? Are any of the records any good or is it all just commercial stuff?*

AD: I'm not but they can be great.

PT: *How do you store your records to keep them in good nick?*

AD: I used to be terrible and then fell in love with a Virgo, who's also one of the world's best DJs. I now behave myself and toplock all records and put classics in plastic sleeves.

PT: *Is everything you buy on vinyl or do you buy CDs too?*

AD: I only buy albums on CD. I do get sent some singles and re-edits on CD but always prefer to play vinyl.

PT: *What's your most prized piece of vinyl?*

AD: Impossible question. I think it fluctuates, but couldn't say.

PT: *Can you tell when you listen to a record for the first time whether it's going to set the dancefloor alight or do you have to try it out on people first?*

AD: Sometimes there's a tune that you instantly know what reaction you'll get depending on how you programme it. But, there are some tunes you just don't get unless you hear them on a great sound system from start to finish, you suddenly lock in and so do a shitload of other people. I like that. It's all down to the programming though, get it wrong and nobody gets it.

PT: *So how did you become a DJ?*

AD: DJing was a natural and unnatural evolution for me. I had been brought up surrounded by music and had spent a large proportion of my formative years in a band's recording studio and learning to play drums. I was always involved somehow in music, loads of different bands when I was in school and then session work, but it had always been a blues, motown, soul and rock upbringing – dance was for cheesy rave kids in tracksuits and dungarees. When I went to university I was without my kit for the first year and was fully exposed to this 'clubbin'' thing and saw DJs mixing for the first time. Being a very novice producer and loving beats I was more than intrigued and had to give it a go. What a piece of piss. When you play drums you're coordinating four different rhythms with four different limbs. Beat mixing doesn't really impress me. It's the people who understand those subtle intricacies, really know the record and above all else, feel it. Those are the best DJs. That whole cut'em'up quick bollocks is for students and big beat types with records that are so boring, that that is what you have to do to stop every knucklehead from leaving the floor to sniff more glue.

PT: *Did you always want to DJ?*

AD: Nope, would have rather died slowly (rock kids didn't like the discotheque). Never considered it. Not until I left my drum kit at home anyway. Now I couldn't be without it.

PT: *What's your background then?*

AD: I'm from the middle of nowhere in the middle of the countryside in the middle of England. It's a hamlet called Milwich that has no shops, not even a post office, but a church and five pubs. Just figure that one out! My family and I were never really a part of the community. I'd always wanted to be a drummer and very nearly went out to LA with a top rock manager but was persuaded to go to Uni instead, at least first and this is how I got into dance culture. However, as much as I loved the energy of the better house tunes around there was still too much sampled rubbish out there (and still is) and I really first got into classics and more downbeat stuff, especially reggae and its varied delights.

PT: *How did Sleaze Nation come about?*

AD: *Sleaze* was born out of a shared frustration my best friend and I had at the time (1996) where we hated our jobs (corporate cack), loved music, London's sub-culture and felt nobody honestly represented what was really happening out there and all this manufactured bullshit had, was and still is dominating the media channels. We rebelled against this, got drunk, resigned and started up *Sleaze Nation*. It's been nuts ever since. People loved the way nobody was safe from a bit of honest feedback and amusing, irreverent critique wrapped up in a stylish package. Within a year it went news-stand in London and within a

71

further six months the good work was being spread in another 30-odd countries. Today it's heralded as one of the world's top fashion titles. *Jockey Slut* started life in Manchester about 10 years ago in a similar way to how *Sleaze* started. Two guys (Johnno Burgess and Paul Benney) wanted to make a difference and started handing out a photocopied A4 sheet called *Jockey Slut*. We'd always loved the mag and it shared so many core values to *Sleaze*; irreverent, amusing, honest and absolutely on it. We purchased the mag in 1998 and it's now regarded as the best dance music mag on the planet. Since then we've recently launched a new mag called *X-Ray* with Xfm that has beaten *NME* (closest competitor) on its first issue and does all sorts of evil things like consult for big brands, manage artists, release records, etc. Lots more to do . . .

PT: *What about the DJing side?*

AD: DJ-wise I had been playing and hardcore collecting since 1992 (I'm 28) and had come out of the bedroom almost immediately because I'd always been involved in music anyway. I'd also promoted various nights and parties before *Sleaze* but once it launched the whole DJ career skipped a few development procedures and CV-building gigs. It was a bit like somebody who'd been DJing for years and then putting a record out, you're suddenly taken more seriously because more people have heard of your name. I used to manage Street Corner Symphony and was co-resident at the Street Corner gig we used to do on a Wednesday night. The club only held about 150 people but we used to have DJs like Cosmo, Ashley Beedle, Chris Rhythm Doctor rocking the place with us every week. I've done quite a few reggae residencies with the Ready When You Ready crew, still play as a resident guest (whatever that is!) with Deep Blue in Copenhagen and co-managed The Bays (one of the hottest dance acts for years) for a while. As a guest I've played lots of great places, highlights being Tenax (Florence), Blue Note (Hoxton, back in the day), played headline stages at festivals with the likes of Chemical Brothers, Rust (Copenhagen), Quart festival (Norway), Headman (Zurich), etc.

PT: *Do you have any horror stories about having a prized record smashed by someone?*

AD: The only real memory of this was coming back from Barbados with Glen Gunner and some other mates. We'd heard this one tune in a supermarket (they have some big systems in supermarkets out there) and ended up finding out what it was, where the record shops were, getting there and eventually managed to bring back two copies that we were going to share. So, I was the first to play a gig when we got back and took this valued piece of plastic with me along with my brand new headphones. At the time I was sponsored by Absinthe and they delivered a few cases of the evil drink to me at each venue I played. Needless to say the party was nuts. When I went to leave I was faced with slippery, wooden stairs that my feet seemed unfeasibly large for. I woke up at the bottom of the stairs with cuts, bruises, broken headphones and only one broken record. My friends still don't believe that's what happened to it.

It was a weight off my mind to find that even Adam, despite all his DJing, publishing and rock credentials, had found shopping for records nerve-wracking to begin with. Armed with his tips I felt brave enough to return once more to the vinyl shops of Berwick Street and the West End. I took a deep breath and wandered into my first port of call – second-hand record store Reckless Records. Reckless actually has two different shops within a few yards of each other – one for dance music and the other for rock'n'roll and Eighties stuff. To ease myself into it I decided to go for the rock'n'roll outlet first and wandered downstairs. It was like being in a sweet shop. They had so much stuff I'd wanted for years and it was all so cheap – from £2 to £5 for an album – all because it was second-hand.

I thumbed through the displays, grabbing some old soul favourites with delight. First I found Dusty Springfield's *Greatest Hits* – for the tracks 'Son Of A Preacher Man' made popular again by *Pulp Fiction* and 'The Look Of Love'. Then I came across a special edition LP of *Give Me Some Loving* by The Spencer Davis Group (that thumping bass always got me jumping around the house when it came on the radio). The icing on the cake was the 12 inch of 'Slave To The Rhythm' by Grace Jones. One of my favourite tunes in the world ever! I hugged them greedily and took them to the counter where I stood nervously fiddling with the record sleeves, waiting for the assistant to eyeball me. A huge black and white photo of diminutive Sixties pop poppet Adam Faith bore ominously down upon me from the ceiling above the counter. To my surprise the assistant was actually pleasant and helpful, remarking that The Spencer Davis Group album was a collector's item and telling me to check for scratches. I marched out of the door with my bag of purchases, narrowly escaping buying the new-ish Fall album at the time – *Are Your Are Missing Winner* [*sic*].

I slipped guiltily into the Reckless dance music outlet a couple of doors down, but when I reflected on how much money I'd saved buying second hand I felt more confident. After spending more than half an hour checking out their wares I bought 'This Beat Is Technotronic' by Technotronic – one of my flatmate Nina's favourites – and beat a path to Piccadilly Circus where HMV, Virgin and Tower Records were all within easy reach of each other. It was a bit less personal there compared to the Berwick Street stores but they had all the latest releases. I hovered about the hiphop section, feeling slightly self-conscious until the obligatory guy in the bandanna complete with hipster wearing side-chick had moved on, and picked up 'I Just Wanna Love U (Give It To Me)' by Jay-Z – something I'd been dying to get for ages. I couldn't wait to get home and listen to it and was beside myself later when I put it on my turntables for a virgin play and found it was warped. Incidentally it's interesting that I've only ever bought one record second hand that's been scratched and at least three brand new from the major record stores that have been warped. Some of the DJs I've spoken to about this say it's all down to the cheap way vinyl is often made nowadays.

With Adam's help I had completed my initiation as a full-fledged record shopper. But as I stood outside Tower Records that afternoon – watching the other wannabe DJs stroll past with their bulging shopping bags – I wondered if I would ever find the courage to play my purchases outside the four damp walls of my Tottenham bedroom.

5

Leaving The Bedroom:
Playing At A Venue

When I bumped into an old mate of mine from university and she said she knew a guy who would let me mess around playing a few records in his bar I couldn't believe my luck. After all, I'd bought my decks humbly believing no one in their right mind would ever let me out of my bedroom to play anywhere. Six months had passed and my mixing was still ropey at best and for the most part non-existent, but I was itching to leave the bedroom and get the feel of playing in a real venue.

When she told me the bar was in Old Street I felt goosebumps of nervous excitement running up and down my back. Old Street in the East End of London – also known as Hoxton – has over the last few years become the essence of DJ trendiness, with its dark rainy streets filled with noodle bars and nightclubs fashioned from disused warehouses. Hoxton is probably to the London DJing scene now what Grimsby is to fish filleting.

It was clear that I wasn't going to be remunerated for my skills as Kevin who ran the bar was doing me a big favour by letting me play at all. I was, however, going to have to play for a mind-blowing four hour set which was no mean feat considering I was used to playing for intervals of half an hour in my bedroom in between tea breaks. But then the buzz from the bar crowd would surely make it all worthwhile, wouldn't it? Little did I know . . .

Besides worrying about what exactly to play – presumably my entire record collection from Goldie to Isaac Hayes in order to pad out four hours – my main concern was how I would fit in loo breaks bearing in mind my appallingly weak bladder. Luckily I remembered my trusty – not to mention sleazy – Donna Summer track 'Love To Love You Baby' lasts about 17 minutes, which was more than enough time to allow me to relieve myself at my leisure.

What my friend had failed to mention was that I was now resident DJ at Old Street's Invisible Bar. Dully painted on the outside and funky on the inside it was the ideal venue for a private party but the people of Hoxton walked past it every day without noticing it was there. The bar was in a fairly prominent location, opposite a popular restaurant and five minutes from the Tube station but the place could have been an old people's home for all the public knew. It was like DJing in the Tardis. Even when Kevin painted the outside bright red and wrote 'BAR' in huge letters no punter came near. The place should have been given the Guinness World Record for being the only empty bar in Old Street.

It was probably a good place to learn, however, as Kevin, a DJ himself, was – despite having also been a boxer – very chilled and laid-back. Plus there was never more than about three punters in the bar at once and they never stayed long enough to complain about the music. Kevin's decks were also an object of curiosity because they were shiny Vestax decks. I found to my new-found technogeek delight that on a Vestax you could put the record into reverse but despite this distraction I remained true in my heart to my trusty Technics 1210s.

Not having a car, one major difficulty I hadn't envisaged was just how difficult it was lugging 60 heavy records around in a shoulder bag and how vulnerable it made you. No one in their right mind would want to be found wandering around in the wee small hours in dodgy Tottenham with their entire record collection on them. You were simply a mugger's delight. Being out of work I didn't have the cash for a set of wheels and I could barely afford a minicab.

Then I hit on a neat and novel solution. I invested in a cheap shopping trolley – one of the ones you see old grannies dragging about Sainsbury's. It wasn't glam by any means and didn't exactly scream DJ at you but that was exactly what I wanted. I could fit all my records in it and hopefully no would-be mugger would have a clue that this shabby looking trolley contained a prized record collection.

To combat the four-hour toilet-free sessions at the bar I recruited my flatmate's boyfriend Alastair – otherwise known as 'A' – to alternate my sets of Sixties soul and Seventies funk (no – I *still* couldn't quite mix) with his exotic offerings of afrobeat records such as the legendary Fela Kuti. One was an 18-minute track featuring the entire commentary of an African football game. Strange days.

Ever the optimists, we attempted to start up our own night imaginatively entitled 'Refreshment', which we advertised with colourful flyers. Naturally – given the venue and our hopeless marketing skills – it flopped unceremoniously on its arse. It wasn't clear to us what exactly the problem or problems were but a combination of them ensured the night bombed. Obviously the venue being an 'invisible bar' was the main obstacle but were we playing the right music in the right order to entice the punters?

It was time to call in the experts once more. Mark Doyle heads up highly successful record label Hed Kandi, set up by London based radio station Jazz FM. He has been DJing since the age of

17 and, as much of his job consists of hunting down records from all over Europe to include on the Hed Kandi compilation CDs, he knows a thing or two about putting a set together. In his messy little office above the Jazz FM studios, tucked away in an unassumingly quiet street off the Edgware Road and over-flowing with myriad CDs and records, Mark explained how to decide what to play and how to get the crowd on your side. He also gave the lowdown on a few highpoints and – especially of interest – the lowpoints of his DJing career.

PT: *How did Hed Kandi come about?*

MD: Hed Kandi was set up about four years ago. It came from myself working here at Jazz FM, running their record label, which was very much a soul and jazz label based on what they were playing on the radio. They gave me the opportunity to compile my own CD on Jazz FM records. It was like a red rag to a bull because they'd been very sensible, very serious – it's Jazz FM and soul music and so forth but I'd had this ongoing career as a DJ running club nights. I'd been DJing since I was 17 years old – all the school discos I used to do and when you'd been a DJ choosing records that people might want to listen to, putting them on to a CD is really just a natural extension of what you do in a nightclub. You're just choosing the very best records for people to enjoy at a particular time or a particular mood and you can be a little more flexible on a CD because you're not trying to keep them dancing for two hours. So I did a CD for them and I was still being quite well behaved because it was still in the mould of Jazz FM but it featured more commercial stuff – like Jamiroquai, some hiphop and a little bit of R&B, a nice mixture of soulful grooves. We called it 'new cool' – it was all about bar culture, listening to cool music in bars and it sold really well.

This was about four years ago. It did extremely well

compared to the more obscure stuff they were doing as a Jazz FM label. And they said, "It sells well but it's not what we do on the station though," and I said, "Well, there's no reason why you can't have another record label that isn't what the station does. It can have touch points, it can be related but be something completely new." And they said, "Right then, off you go then!"

PT: *Where did the name Hed Kandi come from?*

MD: I had this idea knocking around in my head – it was going to be a club night actually – that's where hed kandi came from. You have the eye candy which is the nice girls to look at, and ear candy which is the music and it's all very touchy feely – you can have a club which is hed kandi – as most of your senses are located in your head. I used that name for the label and wanted to do something that was very high quality.

PT: *What's your philosophy behind the label?*

MD: I wanted to go back to the grass roots of compilations, which was you bought Street Sounds which was a big compilation label and it had the best records on it – unmixed full 12 inch versions. And that's what we did – we said Hed Kandi's going to cover a broad spectrum of music – it's going to be music for different points in the day so your disco kandi might be for when you're going out at night, you're beach house is when you're listening during the day and it really builds from having DJed to lots of different audiences, lots of different clubs, having to do the worst wedding disco in the world ever to the trendiest club in Ibiza and it gives you a huge spectrum of music and moods to choose from.

One of the problems with DJs today is that the love of music comes second, the wanting to be a DJ comes first. It's "I want to be a DJ and I'm going to play *that* sort of music." It's fine for certain things but that's a very narrow view and you know the best DJs and the DJs that are around the longest and are still around are the ones that open their ears to everything. As soon as someone says to me, "Oh you wouldn't like that," I say, "You don't know what I like!" I've got AC/DC records in my collection thank you very much!

I think the secret of being a really good DJ or making a really good compilation is to listen to everything to decide what *you* like without being affected by what other people say you should like – what you think is cool – and this is everything we base the label on. It sits between being really cool but also really commercial. If you listen to a disco kandi not only has it got the latest hottest 12 inch release on from Defective Records but right at the end of it there's a completely party anthem version of Lighthouse Family 'High'. That's where Hed Kandi came from. It's been rolling along ever since and the graphics and philosophy mean it's sold all over the world now. You couldn't actually sit down in a room with five marketing people and come up with a brand like this that's got where it is now.

PT: *How do you choose the tracks?*

MD: I put the music on it that I like. That's a prerequisite for everything that goes on a Hed Kandi – would I buy this CD, do I like the record? We're a small team here, we're very accountable so if I put a dodgy record on I take the responsibility. And it just leads to huge nail-biting. That Lighthouse Family record – will they think I'm not cool if I put it on? You listen to everything. And welcome to my desk – (*which is very messy and covered in records!*) this is what I do all day. I'm a complete music obsessive. Every record that comes into the office I listen to, every

CD. Ninety per cent of it gets put in the bin. There's an awful lot of bad music out there – music that's not suitable for us. But for every 10 records you listen to, one will just be the one that goes, "Yeah." And I've got a system where we roughly know what records we'll release in a year, so I've got myself organised and when something catches your ear it's like, "Oh, what would that be right for?"

You get people sending things in saying, "Oh yes, this is *definitely* a beach house record, this is a disco kandi record, this one." We're in a very good position because we've got the radio show and because we're a successful label you get sent an awful lot of music. By the same token the people who have budgets to send lots of music out are generally the people with the most commercial, bad records. And you get piles of stuff from very big mailing houses and it's like, "Oh no!" So as a result I still go out every week and spend going on for £100 to £200 on records.

PT: *Where do you go record shopping?*

MD: Everywhere from HMV in Oxford Circus to Black Market Records to Uptown Records. That's the good thing about working in London – you say, "I'm going for a wander," and you just wander around record shops and pick stuff up. Going abroad to do lots of gigs you spend lots of time in hotel rooms watching local MTV channels, or their local dance channels and you'll see there's records we've picked up for the compilations. We've been in Germany and heard a record and just thought that's great and you ring up the German record label and it won't be released in England at all. OK, we'll pick that up for our compilation.

We've just signed an artist album – something that I heard a year and a half ago in a hotel room in Amsterdam – which was a group called Bastion. They released an album in the Netherlands that never got picked up anywhere else in the world. I drive people mad. I walk past a record shop and I disappear. They're walking up the street talking about something and say, "Where's Mark? Oh there's a record shop right, he's in there." My girlfriend and handbags is the only thing I would compare it to. It's like, oh, I haven't got that one! You don't need another one! Just to keep her happy I take her to Thailand every so often – here, look, lots of fake handbags – have them! Now I'll get my records!

PT: *How do you remember it all?!*

MD: We set up a schedule for the records we want to release through the year and you keep it all in your head. I've got one of those memories where I'm terrible with people's names, Fred, but I could sing you all the lyrics to a record from 1987, I don't have a clue why. And it's like a big category, you listen to something and if it fits you keep a note of it in your head and put it on the next album.

PT: *What advice do you have for a DJ putting their first set together?*

MD: There's two sorts of DJs. There are DJs who can be booked into virtually any situation and still entertain a crowd – and then there are DJs that have a particular sound and there's nothing wrong with being either. I personally go towards the first one – stick me in a room full of 60-year-olds and they can still have a good time because I like the diversity of music and I buy everything. But the realistic side of that is if you're on a limited budget sometimes you have to pick a niche and just focus on those records. It's then more difficult to find work because there's only so many avenues for that sort of music. If you just want to entertain there is work out there. It may not be the work that you want to do ideally. There's always going to be the person who does one gig a month and maybe if they get the break maybe they'll be found and be a superstar. I personally subscribe to the idea that money makes money, and the more money you earn the more you can push yourself.

PT: *How did you get started as a DJ?*

MD: At one point I was running one of the coolest and trendiest clubs in West London. It was a Thursday night in 1988. We walked into an empty bar and said can we do a party here for our friends? And the manager went, "All right then." Then we did it – we didn't have a clue what we were doing but 200 people turned up and the manager said, "Oh you can do this again on a weekly basis, thank you very much." And at that point it was like, "Oh wow, world on a plate, I'm going to be a big DJ, fantastic." We did that for two years but I was very young and didn't really know what I was doing. The scene moves – you're flavour of the month and then people go some-where else. And I really thought, it's the best thing, best night, best effort put into it, they'll all come to it but they didn't – they went to the bigger one down the road because everyone else thought that one far cooler. So I proceeded to lose quite a lot of money, which was a very good learning curve.

PT: *Were you hiring the place yourself?*

MD: I was hiring the place out, putting on other DJs, doing all the printing for the flyers and I managed to – it was only a small venue – but I managed to get myself £20,000 in debt by the age of 21 with a mortgage because the club had been doing so well that me and my brother bought a house. What that taught me was it can all go away tomorrow and I went back and I DJed everywhere. I did horrible bars, I did karaoke nights, I did everything. For whatever reason a DJ is only as good as his records and being able to buy those records every week and keep up with them, because there is so much music out there and if you miss a few weeks and you haven't got *that* record – the crowd go away and you never see them again. You need to keep DJing, practising and it teaches you all different crowds. It does teach you to be a little bit more humble and realise that as a DJ – regardless of how cool, how trendy, or anything else – those people have come to the bar or club and paid anything from a few quid to twenty quid to be entertained. End of story. That's your job. Don't get up your arse about it – "I'm going to take you on a journey and I'm going to teach you the meaning of house music." Bollocks! Play me a record that I can dance to, thank you very much. And that's my philosophy – it's all got a bit too fucking serious.

PT: *What do you make of the cult of the DJ?*

MD : DJs aren't musicians, we play other people's records. Yes, there's great technology out there, which means we can fiddle around with things and some DJs can almost become musicians with the tools at their disposal but the majority of DJs will be those blokes playing other people's records one after the other and to suddenly think, oh, you're Robbie Williams – this is not true and certainly that whole cult of the DJ to a certain extent is over now. There are some very great, big DJs but clubs get *this* big, DJs get even bigger, club has to pay £10,000 to get DJ to club, club can't afford to pay that DJ every week and therefore DJ works somewhere else, there's no loyalty to the club night, it's more to the DJ.

Ultimately even if a DJ's got a huge following if the club

night dies the DJ's got nowhere to play. Clubs haven't been able to keep those DJs because their fees have escalated so much they're working in America now. Clubs are going back to being able to just pay reasonable rates for good DJs and do other things.

At the last club night we did we had drag queens, snow, Father Christmas, two rooms of music, amazing lights, fireworks and those are things you can't afford to do if you're giving someone 10 grand and flying them in on business class. So it's a very good time to be a DJ because it's going to be about good DJs playing good music for the people that want to hear it rather than, "I've read about you in 52 magazines so you must be good. Here, have a large cheque."

PT: *What should budding DJs do to promote themselves?*

MD : Get out there and get yourself noticed. And if that means you do lots of horrendous gigs you don't really want to do, that's what I did. I used the money I was earning from doing all these really terrible gigs – where I was playing not what I normally enjoyed doing – to hire a club and do a night that was free. It took all the stress out of it – I'm going to use this money, pay for the club and I'll invite who I like, they don't have to pay and it'll be an invitation-only thing and that way I get all the people that I actually want to get in the club to the club because it's free and it's a personal invite and then I can play the music I want to. And that's how I got back to doing what I wanted to do again.

It's a case of doing anything you can to play. I've had no money in my pocket and got on buses with two boxes of records – I had to get three buses from where I lived all the way to Richmond to a little bar that wouldn't pay me but would let me play on Tuesday. It ended up as a cool thing. I was doing two other really dodgy things but this cool bar I could afford to do because the other things were paying for it. I didn't have any money to get a cab there so I used to get on a bus and then I'd leave this bar at 11.30 at night after working all day and get back on the bus and have an hour and a half journey home. And then walk with two record bags in the freezing cold. There are those stories where you play two records and a guy comes up to you and offers you a residency but most of the time it doesn't happen like that.

PT: *It's hard graft?*

MD : It's down to hard work and getting yourself out there and playing music all the time. Wherever you can. Having your mum's 50th birthday party – get down there and play the records! For the things that you really hate doing make sure you're paid really well – then you can do the things you love.

PT: *If you've got a four-hour set, how do you divide it up with light and shade?*

MD: I would probably be the worst example to base any technique on because I have a complete shove records in bag, take to club, panic over which record to play next philosophy even after 15 years. You can have a rough idea of what you're going to play and generally on a graph it would be start down there and end up up there. Or you could start up there and bring 'em down again and bring 'em up. It's very difficult to judge. You generally decide the right sort of records that you want to play for a night and it's also down to how successful you are. About three years ago I would have had three times as many records because you need to be a bit more flexible, because they're like, "I want this, I want that."

As people get to know you they get to know your style of music and you gradually can refine your selection. But when you're unknown you still have to be flexible with your crowd because they don't know what to expect, you don't know what they're expecting so you might want to throw some of those extra records in just in case. But at the moment, like last Saturday I knew who was working before me, I knew what sort of music they would be playing and I knew roughly at what point in the night they would finish up. I'm playing one 'til three, it's a prime-time slot, they're not getting tired so you can be really up without being really banging. Look at the overall night, see who else is playing, get an idea of what they'll be playing and slot yourself into what you think is right for that audience. You start off with some nice vocal bits people know and you gradually wind them up and wind them up, and then you have a few big ones and you bring it down again and then another couple of big ones and always finish with a huge massive one the other DJ can't mix into because that really irritates them!

PT: *Do you do that at Hed Kandi nights?!*

MD: We're all quite friendly at everything we do, we always use our family of DJs and we have this thing which is, Get out of that one! I once left 'Club Tropicana' playing on the CD player – a new dance version of it – and we were in Ibiza and it was all very Balearic and "weeeeh", and the DJs busy going, "No don't!" and there it is just going up and up and up. And then it just finished and he said, "You absolute bastard, what am I going to do now?" You just make sure you've got enough records in your bag to provide that light and shade and those big points and always have what I call rescue records, which is like you're playing and it's a little bit flat, ah . . . hang on a minute. Big rescue records of this year would be Tim Deluxe 'It Just Won't

Do'. Put that on, everyone's "raaaaaghhgh" – thank you I'm alive again. That gives you another three unknown records grace if you like before you have to bring them back again, and it's a game where you don't just get lost in your bag and you don't get lost in your mixing.

PT: *What about the crowd dynamics?*

MD: You constantly have to watch people and their faces and watch the crowd and that's the best indication of what you should be doing. In a big club it's quite difficult because you've got even more people to deal with. The stuff we do we generally like rooms of 500 to 800 people. Anything over a thousand and the music gets dictated by how many people you have in the room. Big flouncy housey vocal stuff doesn't work for 2,000 people, it's got to be a bit more "rooooaaaghh", it's got to be a bit darker, a bit harder and they've all got to run on the spot for a little bit longer. The more you've got in a room the harder it becomes to maintain an atmosphere. It's like a law of disappearing averages. You get a little crowd in a room of 50 people, you can play them anything and it's like hysteria but that begins to dissipate over that many people and you're always going to get people who aren't quite into it, aren't into that style. It's being aware of everything – the club, the DJs in there, the crowd, what they're coming for, what records you've got, what you actually want to achieve, what records you want to play and they might not be ones that people know. You've got to mix things up in records that they do know. It depends on the style of night. We do much more commercial nights so it's a lot easier. It's not about other really trendy clubs where it's really obscure and lots of trainspotters all looking over the top. People we play music to just want to party and go "YEAHH" so it's very easy to go, "Yeah, that record."

PT: *How is it with smaller crowds?*

MD: You're on a constant roller coaster in a big club. And then you get nights where you're just doing 250 people in a bar. We do one in Newcastle at a bar called Stereo and it is the most hysteric room – people are carried out in ambulances. You can do no wrong. Put on a record and it could be Zippy, George and Bungle doing 'The Rainbow Song' and they just go "ragghhhh". And it's those points that you're just watching the crowd and you go, "I could get away with anything now," and that's a great feeling because now's the time you're going to pull out that record that maybe you wouldn't normally play. That's when your dodgy remix of, for instance, I've just got a remix of the Stereophonics 'Have A Nice Day' – fucking great, but there's only certain times in the night you could ever get away with it. If you just played it and went, "Yeah, this is a really good dance record," everyone would be, "No." But play it just as they reach that peak where they're all just out of control and they all just go, "Ahhhh yes!"

So it's very much the crowd that you watch, looking at their faces – are they hysterical now? Have you been doing this to them too long, because keep doing it to them and they *will* explode. Sometimes I paint myself into corners where I'm DJing and it's in an hour and it's all going mad and you're up here somewhere at 100 on the scale and there's nowhere to go – "Oh no, what do I put on next?!" The easiest way is to watch other people when you're at home and you play them a record. We play records in the office and people come in and say, "What's that?" Oh, big tune. The best barometer for the mass population of clubbing is the people that aren't huge clubbers because they're people that just want to hear a good record. Like my mother – she's great. She'll say, "Oh I like that record on disco kandi," and sure enough it's the one that goes to number one.

PT: *Would you ever try out a record in a club when you'd never played it to anyone before?*

MD: If you've got enough work you try it out in a small bar you're working at beforehand. It's always a lot easier to deal with 10 people walking off in small bar than 800 people walking off the dancefloor of Pacha. It's like Russian Roulette. With the stuff that we do we get lots of opportunities to do stuff in smaller venues or try things out. It's much better to try things out in foreign countries because (a) they don't know what they're dancing to because they don't speak English – "What is zis song, I do not know?" but (b) it's a lot easier being slated for clearing a dancefloor when it's Poland.

There will always be records that you'll hear and you'll think will work and there'll always be disasters. It's not down to how good you are as a DJ or anything else. It could be just that one night that record will make everyone go "AGGHH" and another night that record will make everyone go, "I'm going in the other room now, thanks very much." You're dealing with music and it's a very subjective, emotional thing and it's down to other people's perceptions. Whether they've had a row with their girlfriend two minutes before or that record particularly reminds them of an ex-girlfriend that they really loved. It's a hundred and one things and that's the great thing about music – it does cause emotion in people. There's always somebody who wants to hear something new. You should always try new music but in the realms of safety. Have your rescue record ready. I hate people who completely clear the dancefloor but because they put the record on they refuse to mix out of it for seven minutes. "I put it on and I'm going to play it." Do anything to get out of it! Get them back!

PT: *How have* you *screwed up?*

MD: I've done everything from take the needle off the record, to a basic thing when you have two records with the same record label playing on both decks and you go, I'll just take that one off, and it's oh dear, that's the one that was playing. To the point where at Pacha last week I was playing a huge record, end of my set, everyone mad, hands in the air and I'm just clearing up all of my records and boom I ejected the CD that was playing. Aagghh, and we couldn't get it back in the CD player and you know what, people aren't that up their arse and I just went, "I'm a wanker – thank you!" Don't take yourself seriously. The crowd very much pick up on what the DJ is doing. It's not just down to their music, it's part of the atmosphere. A serious frowny DJ isn't that much fun. Our DJs are jumping around, you're dancing in the booth and having a really good time and that then comes through. It's very infectious and you don't realise that as much as you're looking at the crowd to see what they want, they're looking at you to see and you're not supposed to go disappearing up your own arse but they do get a vibe off you.

PT: *I once went to this electro night in Old Street and the DJ wore this big puffy jacket and dark glasses and when he played a record he just stood there with his arms folded looking really bored. The music was great and everyone was dancing but then when they saw him they stopped because they thought maybe they shouldn't. It was really odd.*

MD: The trendy thing about Old Street is it's not so much about the music but the whole scene itself and you know I'm just a big housey-disco-spangley-handbag-queen-type person. The good thing is there's something for everyone in music and if you want to be the most up-your-bottom-electrogeeky-dingy club that's really cool because these two magazines write about it but they're the magazines you can only get at these two particular shops then you can.

PT: *Have you had any real disasters?*

MD: Oh I've had a million and one. You name it, it's happened. Drink in the mixer. The best one is the Technics deck – not many people know this but the little on and off thing on the Technics, underneath that twisty thing there's a little hook and it goes from a little eye and turning that thing makes it go on and off but if you turn it the wrong way or flick it or whatever that hook can come out and you end up with this thing in your hand. There's this little hydraulic thing and it stays there long enough for you to realise what you've done and then it disappears into a little housing. It's one of those things where you go, "Oh fuck," and there is no way of getting it out. You have to take the thing apart and there's no way of turning it on then so your deck is fucked. I did that in a club and I had to work with one deck for the rest of the night.

Ex-girlfriends and nightclubs. Bad idea. Always arguments. And the last thing you want to do is have an argument with your girlfriend and have her throw a drink over you which ends up in the mixer. And you then face the audience because the whole mixer has gone 'beeeeehp' and there's no music and 300 people just looked at me like that with coke dripping down my face. The good thing about some mixers that I found is you can actually turn them upside down, shake them out, give them a couple of minutes and they dry and they work again. Zytronic mixers particularly – if you do have slightly psychotic girlfriends a Zytronic mixer is a good mixer to work with.

Then there's disasters like going on gigs and not being paid for them. If you get booked to do anything abroad it's always good to have an agent because we've done three gigs now, even at our level, where we haven't been paid. I went all the way to Australia for two weeks, did four gigs. We knew there was a problem when we got on the plane and we didn't have business class tickets. We were in economy class for 30 hours, had to get off the plane and do a party and knew that there was a problem because one of the promoters had hired a bodyguard to look after me. The other guy that he was working with he'd fallen out with and he was trying to keep his partner away from me because the other guy knew that he didn't have the money to pay me, and he didn't want the other guy telling me. And because everything had been promoted in advance, if we'd turned around and said we're not doing this it's not the promoter that the clubbers go after, they don't know that you weren't going to get paid and that it's a nightmare, they just know that Hed Kandi aren't doing the night that they bought tickets for. That was my personal Vietnam. We did about five different gigs in ten days in Australia and New Zealand just flying around, no sleep, lost about a stone, no money and then the 30-hour flight home. It's a learning curve.

Other disaster stories. Never leave your records by a radiator. Keep your records away from your ex-girlfriends . . .

PT: *Was this the same ex-girlfriend?!*

MD: It was actually. It was the end of our relationship when she frisbeed a record at me so hard that I ducked and it hit the wall and shattered. That was the end of my Kylie Minogue 'Shocked By The Power' 12 inch. I was very upset about that at the time. "You broke my records! That's it! We're finished! They're my babies!"

Thanks to Mark Doyle's handy advice I now had a bit more of

an angle on what to play and how to attempt to work a crowd into a musical frenzy. As a result I was able to put my new knowledge into practice when Alastair and I cooked up a veritable rhythmic storm at my flatmate Nina's birthday party. We rocked the house with everything from Fela Kuti to Fatboy Slim – with only one sticky moment when I cleared the floor with an ill-timed Public Enemy favourite of mine, quickly mixed out of into the cheesy safety of Danni Minogue 'Who Do You Love Now'. The invisible bar which Nina hired for the night had never seen so much action. Nina had been panicking for weeks that none of the guests she'd invited via Friends Reunited would show and she would be forced to ring DialAMate on the night. Just in case, Kev the owner stood by the door in readiness to drag random people in off the street to prop up bar sales but no such action was necessary as the guests poured in and strutted their pissed-up stuff downstairs on the dancefloor. It was a triumph. Kev was gobsmacked and forced to hire extra barstaff for the night.

However the existing problem – the er . . . complete absence of any crowd in fact at our little night in Hoxton on a Wednesday evening – continued unabated. It was clear that finding a new marketing strategy and probably a new venue was the only answer.

6

Organising A Club Night And The Joys Of Being Female

After our triumphant night at Nina's birthday bash Alastair and I were still on a DJing high but we dreaded the following Wednesday night down at the Invisible Bar.

"Wasn't it just fantastic when you dropped 'Kinky Afro' in? They really went nuts," was one of the mutual pats on the back I gave A when we arrived down at the venue.

"Yeah but you really got the atmosphere going with your funky set first," A generously replied in the same vein. "They might not have been dancing at that stage because they were still drinking, but you really set them up nicely for my Nineties set."

Kev – the only one of us to have pocketed any hard cash from the hire fee and the overflowing bar sales – was similarly appreciative. "Hey you guys really rocked the place on Saturday night. Anytime you want to have another party just let me know." A and I grinned knowingly at each other and set to work. We couldn't wait to get back on the decks, we were on such a roll and at 7 pm we had the whole night ahead of us.

By 9 pm we were ready to sign a suicide pact. The place was like a morgue on a bank holiday. A strange looking couple were the only punters there when we arrived and even they had departed by 8 pm. In our misery and boredom we speculated that they were having a seedy little affair and had chosen this

Cosmo, alias Colleen Murphy: "It's like when someone waits tables and the kitchen fucks up. Do they go yell at the chef? No, they yell at the waitress. Don't shoot the DJ!"

Scratching legend Cutmaster Swift: "It's a bit like rubbing your stomach and patting your head."

Mark Doyle, of Hed Candi: "The secret of being a really good DJ or making a really good compilation is to listen to everything to decide what *you* like without being affected by what other people say you should like."

Jockey Slut Magazine and *X-Ray* owner Adam Dewhurst: "I love going to old collectors shops in provincial towns. It's not unusual to find a pile of your must have classic records of all time for a few quid. You've got to love a bargain."

Anne Savage: "It sounds awful but most of the girls I knew were more interested in what they were going to wear when they went out and what they were drinking. I was always the nerd by the decks watching the DJ." (© *Idalina/PYMCA*)

Nikki Lucas: "It's so competitive, there's no overtime, there's no free paid holiday, there's no sick pay, nothing. You just work your butt off and smoke lots!"

Graeme Park: "You've got to play to the crowd because otherwise if you don't you're going to have an empty dance floor and also they're not going to come back and see you next time." (© *Gordon Park/PYMCA*)

Smokin' Jo: "A good DJ plays from the heart, you need to feel a passion for what you are playing."

Les Adams, lecturer in the art of DJing at the Academy of Contemporary Music in Guildford: "The secret of staying in this industry and actually making a career out of it is to keep up to date with the music and to be prepared to adapt to new styles."

David Morales, Galaxy FM: "Avoid shady promoters, bullshit wannabe managers/agents and heavy partying."

Radio 1's Dave Pearce: "... love the music you are playing, otherwise it's just a technical exercise and you will never be able to take people on a journey or understand the power of the reaction that certain songs can provoke."

Steve Sutherland, of Galaxy FM DJ, winner of two MOBO Awards for Best DJ:
"DJs... disappear very quickly – so learn how to say please and thank you."

Judge Jules: "There's hardly a DJ out there who earned more from DJing within their first five years than they spent on records."

Luxemburg legend Tony Prince: "It's a much better hobby than clog dancing!"

Roger Sanchez: "The impression is that it's an easy way to get money and women but unfortunately it doesn't come as easy as that. You have to have a true love for the music." (© *Eva Mueller*)

particular venue for their sordid tryst, safe in the knowledge that the place would be deserted. Hot on the heels of our winning turn on the previous Saturday – the ghosts of tunes and dancing drunken feet still in the air – the disappointment was cruelly compounded and what's more we knew we were stuck there for another two hours.

What had gone wrong? We had flyered all the people who came to the party, sent our listing details to *Time Out* and the *Evening Standard*, e-mailed everyone we had ever laid eyes on and flyered the local pubs. Not one friend of ours turned up. Not even Nina, who was busy having a guitar lesson or something. Others were stuck at work or had better places to go. But then it was a school night, being a Wednesday. Until 10.30 when to our disappointment A's friend Amabel arrived – disappointing because by that point we were wishing desperately that no one who knew us would turn up and find us in such a sad and uncool position. A put on a particularly depressing 20-minute African-influenced Joni Mitchell track and the three of us contemplated ending it all with the spare Stanton record needles I'd brought along. Then it dawned on us that since the place was so dead it was unlikely our decomposed corpses would be found for centuries to come.

Maybe the bar was cursed and built on bad ley lines – or maybe our marketing strategy sucked. As women are considered to be better communicators than men, I wondered if DJ Nikki Lucas would be able to shed some light on our marketing failings and put us back on the road to DJ superstardom. Nikki DJs with legendary Afrobeat outfit The Shrine and also DJs at Fabric night club in London. A New Zealander, she is one of the UK's top R&B DJs on the London gay scene and now also runs record label and club night Bitches' Brew with colleague Cosmo (see chapter 2) in Hoxton. I sought her advice on

97

getting a fledgling club night off the ground and couldn't resist asking about what it's like being a female DJ in what is still very much a male-dominated business.

PT: *How should a bedroom DJ go about setting up a first club night?*

NL: What I suggest to anybody is you find an empty bar or warehouse – and you fill it up. It might take a year, it might take two years and you just keep working and working at it. It sounds really crazy but you work for free and either in a collective form or whatever. With virtually all my nights I've set up when I first started that's how I've set everything up. Say there's five, six people – two people doing flyering, one person's on the door, one person's dealing with the mailing list, one person's making sure the things are going to be coming in – two or three DJs. So everything's going to be guest list orientated but the more people helping out the more people they'll be bringing in. Friends will tend to pay a donation because they know how hard you're working and then they'll be spreading the word. It's a simple thing – that's just the basic bit. The other thing that's always important and it has been for me – is locking a loophole in the market.

PT: *Really? What kind of loophole?*

NL: For myself, there was no woman R&B scene. There's a huge R&B scene in the underground but not up in the commercial club scene so there was that loophole for me. The Shrine wasn't really a loophole, The Shrine was more like Fela Kuti (*a hugely influential African musician*) died and we put on a night as a memorial for him and that worked so we thought we'd carry it on. Think about how you want to do it, where you want to go. The interesting thing about DJing is for

98

whatever reason when you start you have to realise you're probably not going to be playing what you really want to be playing. Start trying to set yourself up and see what you think's going to work as a financial thing.

PT: *What about getting in magazine listings?*

NL: If you end up getting a following and people understand what you're doing then you have to let people know what's going on – the media's very important. It's hard work because when you start by yourself who do you know to go to on *Time Out* and who do you know to go to in order to get in different magazines?

PT: *How did you become a DJ?*

NL: I started getting into music when I was eight. I lived in the bush so once a month I used to save my money to buy one seven inch, which would normally be a Motown sort of thing. Then I hit the big city and really got into reggae and punk – that shows how old I am! – back in the Seventies. Back then what we called DJing isn't really what we call DJing now because I played back to back a lot of soul, rock and blues tunes all mixed up and we put on parties. I came to London because I'd got so much into reggae and I was a bass guitar player that I wanted to be in a woman's reggae band and funnily enough it came about. The first week in London I was in a band – all my dreams came true all at once. Then I heard salsa for the first time in my life – I'd never heard salsa before. I didn't know what it was, it just blew me away hearing different stuff. So during the Eighties I actually missed out on the whole house thing. It just went above or below me or all around me but not in my world.

In the Nineties I got really into a lot of jazz. I used to go to house clubs and dance but it was a party thing for me. Then I heard Masters At Work 'I Can't Get No Sleep' and it was one of those changing points for me musically – listening to more house, buying more house and just realising it's not just about house, it's about all sorts of music. Then I was really fortunate enough to meet Rita Ray and Max Reinhardt who are actually my partners who I do The Shrine with and started working a lot with them – more of the global music. I bring in the house and the R&B, hiphop and the ragga influences.

During the same period I set up the first mainstream women only R&B hiphop night that's now the longest running women-only night in London where we became very famous and really on for it. A couple of years ago I set up with a bunch of people a mixed night called Bootilicious which became one of the top five clubs in the country for R&B, hiphop and ragga. Again it's another gay night. I play all over and the music influences are all over. I do The Shrine which is predominantly African, I do a lot of R&B, hiphop nights and then Bitches' Brew which is predominantly house. But then I play everything from African house to soulful house, to some cheese occasionally when I feel like being naughty!

PT: *I suppose there's a few more women DJs now?*

NL: I think London's special in the world because there are actually a lot of women DJs, which is really lovely. Even in New York you go to a women-only club and there's men DJing there because they can't find a woman. That's intriguing for me because it's like, oh my God! I don't know why London women are choosing it more to become a career whereas elsewhere obviously they're not. It's hard wherever you are, whether you're a boy or a girl being a DJ, being into art and music. It's so competitive, there's no overtime, there's no free paid holiday, there's no sick pay, nothing. You just work your butt off and smoke lots!

PT: *Have you got a pension?*

NL: No! Yeah – I'm going to be like Labour says, I ain't going to have a pension. I'm going to have to work 'til I drop.

PT: *The first time you played in a bar or a club was it nerve-wracking?*

NL: Oh, it's always nerve-wracking! It's still now! If you're playing with people who you have always been like "oh my God!" about and then you're playing with them or you're warming up for them it's *still* like "oh my God!" I still shake. But I think it's part of the fun of it though – it makes me work. I have to always prove myself. You have to try not to let things settle where you feel confident. Sometimes I feel really confident and other times I don't. I don't know if that's also partly being a girl as well because we can be like that. Perhaps I should talk to more boys and see if they feel like that too so it's not just a girl thing.

PT: *Women are more critical of themselves.*

NL: I think women are a lot harder on themselves. Also in the business it just amazes me how hard they're working.

PT: *Do you always play records in the same order?*

NL: It depends how it goes. I never really play stuff in the same order. Sometimes I might do similar mixes because I know it's going to fit. It really depends. Some nights it could be that people want it a bit deeper rather than commercial. Especially in

R&B and hiphop, which is completely pop really. If I want to introduce a new tune like Jurassic Five that isn't pop I have to work out how to do that. So it's just planning that out and hoping for the best. If you clear the floor then better start again! I tend to work like that. Sometimes I might play a bit more carefully but generally I don't anymore or I get bored especially with R&B tunes.

PT: *Do you play commercial house?*

NL: On the house scene I play what I play – I don't really compromise. I think it's harder to become a house DJ in London because there's so much house here and everyone's playing the same thing, so if you play something different no one wants to hear it, they all want to hear the same thing. I don't tend to go for those gigs and if people ask me to play then I say, "What do you want? I'm sorry I can't do that because it means I have to go out and buy the music and I'm not into it." I'm fortunate but it's taken me a long time to get to this point because I've done commercial house before and it was awful.

PT: *Can it be quite miserable playing stuff you don't like?*

NL: Playing stuff you don't like and stuff for a crowd that's absolutely awful. Where there's a bunch of blonde haired girls boozing it.

PT: *Do they come over to you and bother you?*

NL: Yeah! The amount of times you get threatened over what you're playing. You know they're not going to do it but you know they're like, "Where's my fuckin' whatever record!"

PT: *Are they like that with male DJs as well?*

NL: I think they are. I don't know. I haven't really talked about it with the boys. Me and Cosmo talk a bit because we do a lot together and we're just like, oh my God here comes one of them. And funnily enough with the boy clubbers it's fiddling with the mixer. You say, "Excuse me, I'm actually working here, who are you? Go and fiddle with *his* knob when he's finished, don't fiddle with my knob." Maybe he hasn't got a knob!

PT: *Do you get other DJs patronising you?*

NL: I think I've been patronised by everyone at the end of the day in some weird way. I think I've been very lucky because I have come from the gay scene where I set up my own night so there's no one I'm playing for and so my name's created because I've created it myself, which is a lot harder work in some ways than if you DJ at the club where you go and you can get the big gigs straight away, which sometimes does happen. Sometimes I do get comments like, "Oh where's the DJ? When's the DJ turning up?" And I say, "In five hours time." At the end of the day I think the industry is so competitive that in some ways it is a bit easier being a woman than a boy. A lot of promoters are saying they prefer having women DJs DJing. They're not over the top as much. But when it's 10 per cent girls and 90 per cent boys you're going to get more bad boys than bad girls. Maybe if it were 50:50 it wouldn't be like that.

At the moment I think it's so competitive for everybody and I think women do have less prominence than men, and women also haven't been so anal about music. Men have been anal since they were babies. They've been fixing their stereos since they were two. In some ways it's more about how you've been brought up than actually about DJing. If you're a DJ and you're supposed to go on, most women will wait whereas a boy DJ will be confident – "I'm playing at midnight, I'm coming on." Which is fine. That's just how it is. But it's that confidence thing again.

PT: *They push themselves forward.*

NL: Boys have been taught to push themselves more.

PT: *What advice would you have for someone starting out?*

NL : You need to work out your market. Get the right market. So if you are doing R&B, work out what the market is for R&B. Or are you doing house, or are you doing world music or Middle Eastern music.

PT: *When you turn up to play do you do a sound check?*

NL: I did used to when I first started because I was really nervous and now I don't. You need to get to know the mixer and sometimes it's quite hard. Like Friday I was playing in the R&B room and then I was going to do half a set in the house room and the mixer was so different I'd never used it before and I fucked up every mix and it freaked me. Again it's that confidence thing. It doesn't matter if you fuck up a mix either because everybody does. It's very important to practise. Two hours a day. One hour a day. Just keep practising and practising. Try and get warm-up sets for someone, if you don't want to set up your own night, but you won't be paid.

PT: *I've been playing four hour sets in this bar and there's never anyone there! Just me and the barman!*

NL: The first thing you need to do is promote and that's the hard part. It's a financial commitment when you get to the next stage because bars never pay. Try and find a Friday or Saturday night and with good people to help you to get past that point. Some people just carry on with not being paid until it gets busier and busier, but again it's up to you to make it get busier and make sure people know what's going on. In some ways it's better to start off with a once a month thing. With your friends you can do once a month – you can't do weekly.

PT: *We found that whilst doing our night in Old Street. Once a week is too much. Friends start off coming but they stop after one or two weeks.*

NL: It's a lot of work. I don't recommend DJing to anyone to be honest!

PT: *And it's odd hours as well, isn't it?*

NL: I used to be a painter and decorator and I used to DJ at night. I'd finish work at six, go and DJ with my mates until 2 am and start work at 8 am the next day.

PT: *Do you need much sleep?*

NL: No. You live on little. DJing's something I just don't recommend to people if they ask me. If you're working full-time you've got finance, you've got security. Save up your money and buy a nightclub! You can have your own night! The first 10 or 15 years you're not going to make any money. Not to live on – all your money's going to go on records.

PT: *Is that how it was for you?*

NL: Yes. It's only the last two years that I've been living off DJing.

PT: *When did you stop painting and decorating?*

NL: I stopped that about five or six years ago. Then I worked in a record shop for three days a week. It was wonderful. If you want to become a DJ go and work in a record shop one or two days a week. You're paid shite but then you're out there. You're meeting people. It won't get you gigs or anything like that but it's a good start.

PT: *What does help you get gigs?*

NL: Work. Hard work. For me demo tapes never worked. For some people tapes work but for me it never has. I think I make shite demos! Go to your favourite club where you think, I really want to play here. You go every week, you get to know the DJs. You say, I just love the music, I really want to play here. That's always worked for me, funny enough. It's a bit of a cheeky "come on let me have a go" thing, in a nice way. Not where you're starting to irritate people. It's also worked for me with my nights. At this R&B night there was this woman who used to come every month and say, "I'd really like to DJ, blah blah blah." Then she started putting on her own nights and suddenly people were saying, "She's really good," so I thought I'd get her down there and get her to warm up and now she's the main DJ. You can always try someone out as a warm-up and if they don't work out you don't invite them back.

PT: *Have you ever had anything go wrong?*

NL: Oh, things go wrong all the time. I went to Poland – Crakow, this town near Auschwitz the other week and there was this wonderful bar. And my mixing jumped and nothing would stop jumping. I looked down and it turned out the floorboards were wobbly. At that point you just have to go with the flow. Or your monitor's not working and you just have to get on the mic and tell people. Most people are fine with it. They just want to know what's happening. This year I was playing at Brighton Mardi Gras and I was spinning and all the rain starts pouring through the tent onto my records and everything's just getting wet. And so I got a few mates to stand around with umbrellas! Some people thought it was my stage image – not realising! So you can always get around it with humour.

PT: *Have you ever turned up with the wrong music for a night?*

NL: Funnily enough I was playing in Moscow at a club called Propaganda and I'd brought African music and it was a house night. And I'm thinking, what the fuck am I going to play? I'd got African house but not enough for the whole night. So I just thought, fuck it I'll start with Fela Kuti. People went crazy, absolutely crazy. Most of the time that works if you're with a crowd that is into music. A lot of house crowds are really into music. But I tend to have a mixture of everything in my bag just in case.

PT: *How many records do you take with you?*

NL: About 100 which pisses me off! I want to have someone – a boy who'll carry my music around for me! But I've got big shoulder muscles now! I feel really privileged that I'm living the life of what I've chosen to live. Would like more money but most of my friends aren't living the life they want to live, are fed up, hate their jobs. If you're into music I think DJing is something you have to do. You have to make that commitment of realising that you have to have some way of supporting yourself while you do it. A partner helps.

PT: *It's a very demanding job, isn't it?*

NL: It *is* a very demanding job. It's not good for relationships and it's not good for keeping friendships either. All of my friends are free over the weekend – I'm busy over the weekend. Having that normality with people is quite difficult sometimes. Some of my best friends I only see once a year, which is crazy.

While I was still really into the music, I couldn't help but be slightly put off by Nikki's tales of DJing gloom – the hard graft, the holding down the day job while DJing at night till all hours – and the saddo financial journalist part of me baulked at the thought of reaching 40 with no pension or financial security of any kind. Not to mention never seeing my friends and spending my weekends lugging my shopping trolley around. It's not a cool, trendy thing to think but what happens if aged 45 my back finally gives out after the years of heavy bag carrying and I can't work and I've got nothing to fall back on apart from my Spencer Davis Group special edition LP of *Give Me Some Loving*?

After listening to Nikki and Mark tell their hard luck stories of starting out as DJs I was struck by how little of this ever seemed to find its way into mainstream club culture. All the cool teenage boys and girls wanting to be the next Roger Sanchez or Lottie were not dreaming of spending 10 years holding down some crappy day job from 8 am to 6 pm every day and then

DJing for nothing in some grotty bar a two-hour bus ride away every night. They dreamt of spinning a couple of records in a trendy Soho nightclub or sending off a demo tape and immediately being discovered. Hotfooting it onto the road of superstardom. But it was clear that this was far from being the reality. Mark was in his thirties – already having been £20,000 in debt from DJing and forced to DJ at all manner of weddings and Bar Mitzvahs in order to repay his debts and claw his way back to success. Nikki too was about to hit 40. But it was also apparent that these people were truly obsessed by music and were driven by some musical demon – as though Orpheus, the mythological musician who made the rocks move, was back tormenting their souls. They weren't DJs because they wanted to be cool, hip, famous or even stinking rich – like priests they had some kind of calling, a true vocation and frankly had no choice in the matter. They had not chosen DJing – DJing had chosen them. The question was, was DJing calling me and if so, considering my extensive credit card debt and precarious financial position, did I really want to listen or frankly leave the message to go to voicemail?

7

Turning Professional

The Collective Tales of DJ Woe as told by seasoned pros Nikki Lucas and Mark Doyle had turned my stomach somewhat and to be frank I was reminded about the time my mother slammed my harebrained university dreams of becoming an actress after landing the lead role in a student production of *The Cherry Orchard*. "You'll be on the dole all the time because you'll hardly ever get any work," she nagged. "And even if you do you'll have to sleep with all the directors to get it and take all your clothes off on screen!" Far away from the fairytale land of bigshots like Pete Tong and Paul Oakenfold, the small-town world of DJing wasn't that different from the miserable society of the wannabe actors in *Withnail And I*.

I pictured myself in ten years' time as a toothless alcoholic sleeping rough in a Hoxton doorway – probably the doorway of the Invisible Bar – having been forced to sell my decks and records for booze but under the duvet fashioned from old fish and chip papers I would still be clutching my beloved 12 inch of 'Slave To The Rhythm' by Grace Jones.

In order to maintain our fragile sanity, A and I pulled the plug on our little failed club night and parted ways with the Invisible Bar. I played a few gigs here and there – one a warm-up set of soulful Seventies classics such as Gil Scott Heron's 'The Bottle' at Andy Weatherall's trendy Fortress Studios in Old Street at a night organised by Kev. The equipment stand for the decks doubled as a pool table. Despite being a sworn rock chick my mate Maxine loyally acted as my groupie/audience.

Sean, a former work colleague of A's who sometimes DJed rare groove at Refreshment while A and I dashed out for some chips, ran a couple of nights at another club in the Old Street area, which was a former strip joint and still had a fantastically sleazy pole in the middle of the dancefloor. In exchange for playing the first hour's warm-up set to an empty room (a purist, Sean tutted at my signature tune 'Slave To The Rhythm') I did the door for the rest of the night, which was not a great deal of fun but certainly an eye opener. I lost count of the people I let in because they insisted they were on the guest list or were related to the club owner or just said I should let them in for less because they were ginger. Needless to say Sean, who had spent a lot of money on hiring the place, failed to break even. Although much of this was probably my fault, it was mainly because there had been a World Cup match earlier in the day and the punters were too pissed and tired to go clubbing. Thankfully the huge friendly bouncer employed by the club relieved my crushing boredom by attempting to chat me up. His technique included, (a) bragging about his four girlfriends (b) explaining how he still lived with his mum and (c) after observing that despite his smooth patter I still had my nose in a book, outlining his enthusiasm for the works of Jackie Collins – "She's really got a way wif words – nah what I mean?"

As the months went on and my bank balance became lighter and lighter, I left the precarious freelance journalism world behind me and joined *Shares Magazine* full-time as a reporter. Soon enough through work I also met a lovely new bloke called Douglas (we met at the romantic setting of a nasal drug delivery conference). Doug – a former indie kid who had grudgingly swapped his combats for a shirt and tie at work – spent a great deal of time attempting to widen my musical tastes to accommodate Green Day, The Lemonheads, Nine Inch Nails and er . . . Natalie Imbruglia – the latter simply because he fancied her. One small obstacle in our relationship was the fact he had lived in Zambia until he was 13 and had entirely missed out on the Eighties music and culture that was so close to my Essex heart. I laughed it off and called it his 'lost decade' but realised that if the relationship were to stay the distance it was something we'd have to work through. I mean, for God's sake the guy hadn't even heard of Spandau Ballet!

Quickly I got sucked back into the familiar routine of juggling work and boyfriend. Although I still loved my decks and music, the call of the DJ demon was now a very quiet voice in the back of my head that could hardly be heard above the tap, tap, tapping of my computer keyboard at work and icky thoughts of romance and coupledom. Maybe DJing wasn't my calling after all and it was just as it began – a way to fill the lonely void and get even with my ex. Then all of a sudden my friend Katherine announced she was getting married and that she wanted me to DJ at the wedding. I hadn't played anywhere for at least three months and wondered if I could still pull it off. DJing for nothing when I was working from home was fine but I'd found that after a long day's work a four-hour set on a school night was no easy slog. But a friend's wedding would be a completely different kettle of fish.

In the event it was a turning point. Katherine's wedding crowd was an eclectic one to say the least. She's a solicitor at a big city firm but hails from Teesside. Her husband Mark is a former Goth (they have matching piercings) and has numerous Goth mates who turned out in force at the registry office in Wandsworth. The reception was awash with black leather, piercings and rubber. Although he failed to wear a suit, one guest was commended for having actually worn shoes and socks to the event, as he was accustomed to going about his business barefoot. "Look, Toby's wearing shoes!" exclaimed one guest. "Ah yes, but this is a municipal building, you know," his companion replied knowingly.

Four sets of parents were also in attendance as both the bride and groom's parents were divorced and had new partners. I looked at my record bag and wondered how the hell I would manage to coax any of these people onto the dancefloor, considering their diverse musical tastes. Alan, another mate of Katherine's and a techno DJ who mixed religiously, was playing after me and had a number of electro records. The old folks wouldn't be into it but the Goth crowd probably would so I figured he had more of a chance. The second problem was my dwindling sobriety. I'd joined the groom's party in the pub before the ceremony and downed a swift vodka, followed by the usual champagne at the reception – in a little bar on High Holborn – and by 5.30 pm we were still waiting for our food. By 6 pm I was slurring my words and laughing too loud. But somewhere along the line a miracle occurred and I wound up with the crowd eating out of my hand. Staggering around in my drunken stupor I played my Sixties soul, the Seventies funk, some Michael Jackson and the next thing I knew they were all up and strutting their drunken stuff. Katherine's dad in his jacket, tie and hushpuppies was happily grooving alongside this tiny Goth girl clad in a turquoise rubber dress, biker boots and complete with chin piercing. Digging through my record bag I found my precious 7 inch of 'D'ya Think I'm Sexy' by Rod Stewart – a personal childhood favourite and cheesy as hell. I'd picked it up for 25p by chance in a charity shop in Lewisham. Did I have the guts to put it on? Oh, what the heck! I put the needle on the record. The crowd went wild and I stood back flabbergasted. I played them Kim Wilde's 'Kids In America', Timo Maas and 'French Kiss' by Lil' Louis and they continued to grind. It was fantastic! In a flash it was as though all those miserable evenings down at the Invisible Bar had happened to somebody else.

Then the cherry on the cake. Mid cueing up, this guy approached me and introduced himself as the bar manager. "God this is great – I haven't heard this stuff for years. How much do you charge? We'd like to book you on a weekly basis."

I couldn't believe my ears. At last, someone wanted to pay me for this.

In my amazement I was unable to give the guy a price but tried to recover my cool by saying I'd get back to him in due course. It was probably a good idea to get the advice of a real professional before turning 'ahem' professional – if you could really call it that. After all, we weren't exactly talking about the big time here. Anne Savage has been DJing since 1990 when the Acid House phenomenon and its illegal raves captured her imagination and made her determined to escape her unhappy home life and become a successful DJ. Readers may remember her from the cult programme 'Faking It' on Channel 4 in which she, alongside fellow mentor Lottie, coached shy cellist Sian to fake it successfully as a DJ. Anne explains how the professional DJ gets gigs, an agent and publicity.

PT: *How did you turn professional, Anne?*

AS: I was always into music from a very early age. I played classical guitar for eight years, then I played in a band. It was nothing serious – just some kids trying to be in a band but then that didn't work out. My friend was a DJ in a bar playing old soul classics and I just thought, shit I want to be a DJ! I asked him to teach me but you can't really teach somebody, you've just got to get two records and learn yourself. Then I managed to blag a gig – even though I couldn't DJ I had a massive record collection, I'd been collecting for years from soul, reggae, New Order, hiphop, all different kinds of music. There used to be a local club where I used to live in Accrington called the Curfew Club and the resident DJ wanted to go on holiday for two weeks so they said OK, you can come and play. I did it and I must have been terrible! I had no idea, I'd never done it before and I'd never seen decks, although I had records. It wasn't a disaster but it wasn't brilliant and at the end of the night two girls came up and said it's great to see a female DJ. So I got a really good response and I thought, shit, maybe I can do this!

About a month later I decided to pack up and move to Italy with my sister and the first club we walked into we got jobs as promotion girls. They let me warm up every night – I mean I had to play Chris Rea and really awful stuff. At the time my sister went back home and sent me these tapes of Acid House and told me there were these illegal raves going on. I came home and she took me to one of the first illegal raves and I turn up in a tailored jacket and shoes. We walked in and there's everyone going mental and I lost her but just had an amazing time and thought, oh my God, I love house music. So I started buying house music and was always the one who used to go to parties and play records. Eventually I managed to persuade the local promoter to book me for his nights. I also used to go to these illegal raves with a bag of records. No one really got paid but you'd wait your turn to play and I was so bad but just determined to do it. Then I thought I'm going to take this seriously and I sat at home just playing two records for about two weeks, practising, practising, until I thought I was good at it. The big club in my hometown was Angel in Burnley and I befriended the promoter and hounded him until eventually he said OK, you've got a residency for £25 a week and you start in two months' time. I didn't have a job at the time so I used to get up at 9 am in the morning and practise. By Wednesday I would work out what records I was going to play and then I would practise what order I was going to play them in and by Saturday I would set the alarm, practise, have a lunch break and go back to it. That's how dedicated I was. I remember my Dad saying to me, "What are you doing?" He thought I was going mad. "Get a job." And I said, "No, I've decided I'm going to be a DJ, I'm going to be the best DJ ever and earn thousands of pounds." And he told me I was mad.

I got the residency and went on like this week in, week out. I used to just play the first two hours. It was ridiculous. People were just walking in – there was hardly anyone there. At the same time all my favourite DJs were playing there like Carl Cox – it was a techno club – and I watched. I was always the one at the side of the decks just watching and learning and thinking, I want to be like them. Eventually they let me have the main slot and I started getting bookings outside the residency and got proper money like £100. Two big promoters in Leeds heard of me and one of their clubs was a mixed gay straight club who did a lot of press so I started getting articles in magazines when I used to play there. Also I started playing at a big rave in Leeds called Arch and I started building up a fan base so people started asking for me at the club and I got booked that way. Once I got a name I managed to persuade an agency to take me on. That's what you need – representation – and they got me bookings.

PT: *At what stage did you think, OK I'm a professional now?*

AS: I always treated it as a job but after a while I did have to get another job because I was only getting £25 a week and I got a job in a record shop. It was unbelievably fantastic because I got to listen to all different types of music. But when I realised that this is full time was when I had enough money to give up the day job and I couldn't maintain the day job because I was working so hard at the weekend.

PT: *What about your mental attitude to DJing as a professional? Does it change?*

AS: It's just the experience of playing in front of a crowd. After a certain amount of time you become more professional – you can read a crowd and you don't get fazed. You could be the greatest DJ in the world in the bedroom but be unable to have the guts to pull that off in front of a massive crowd.

PT: *In your case it sounds like becoming professional happened very quickly.*

AS: Not at all. It was 1990 when I decided I wanted to start DJing and it wasn't until 1993 that I got my first residency. Then it was 1996 when I was taken on by an agency and it all kicked off. I started making records too so that helped. It certainly wasn't overnight.

PT: *It sounds like you were very focused – that's unusual for a girl. It's normally guys that are that anal about DJing!*

AS: It sounds awful but most of the girls I knew were more interested in what they were going to wear when they went out and what they were drinking. I was always the nerd by the decks watching the DJ. To make it as a DJ I think you don't have to just want to be one and want all the fame and success, you genuinely have to love music, that has to be the most important thing. I can't stress it enough. If you don't love music you are not going to make it. It took me years and so many knock-backs.

117

PT: *Like what?*

AS: Like promoters trying to drag me down a dark alley. Driving for miles and not getting paid anything. Treated like shit at times. Not being given a drink the whole time I'm there. Turning up and being told to go away, they don't want me to play. This happened for years – even when I had an agent.

PT: *Seriously! Promoters used to do that?!*

AS: Oh yeah. They'd help you to your car with your records and then it would be, "Is there anything else I can do for you?" and all this shit.

PT: *Was this because you were a woman?*

AS: It was partly because I was female and foolishly I used to go on my own. Sometimes I'd take a load of mates but often I'd be on my own. It takes a lot of determination. It's not easy by any stretch.

PT: *Was there any point when you thought, stuff this, I'm giving up?*

AS: No never. Like many successful people in business or whatever I had something to prove to my Dad. I was the black sheep of the family and I was written off. I couldn't hold a job down, I was just the worst worker. I used to work for my Dad and I must have had ten different jobs. I just didn't want to do that. And so I was going to prove to my Dad that I could do something and that's what drove me to it. I had a really shit time at home so it was about wanting to be liked and wanting to be good at something. There was nothing else I could think of – once I started that was it, I had to do it.

PT: *Is it very important to have management?*

AS: There's other ways you can do it. We tried to start up our own night and I know a lot of DJs who did that – maybe started small and built up a small fan base, spreading the word so people are starting to ask for you in other clubs. Or getting press down to your own night and trying to build on it that way. But to take you to that next level you have to have representation. Definitely. Not just because they're going to get you work but because there's contracts involved and it's so much easier for someone else to negotiate a fee. When I used to do it myself I'd end up saying I'd do it for £50 just because I wanted to do it. I loved it that much I'd drive for miles and it would cost me money.

PT: *Is it difficult to get representation? Do they go to clubs looking for new clients?*

AS: No. They don't go talent spotting. You've just got to hassle them and send them tapes. Every gig that you do, collect a flyer – it's like building a portfolio or a CV. Send it off to an agent, don't be put off if they say no. Leave it a while and keep sending in stuff until they take you on. It's not enough just to be a good bedroom DJ. Because things change so much you've got to have something different now – an angle or in your set not just play the same thing as everyone else. Drop an old tune in your set or have some other skills like scratching. You've got to be really something to get through these days. There's so many DJs. The younger generation of DJs that are coming through are so good. I think a lot of early DJs got away with not being too good at mixing purely because they got so much press. Everyone reads the magazines and believes what they read and goes to see them. The press can create a monster really. These days, technical skills are paramount.

PT: *Why is that?*

AS: It's because everyone's got decks at home. Guaranteed if I go to play at a gig 50 per cent of kids in the crowd will have decks and know how to mix and won't stand for it. I've played at Essentials in Birmingham and I won't name names but if a DJ wasn't good the crowd will just sit on the floor with their arms folded and won't dance. Can you imagine anything being more terrifying than that and it's happened to quite a few big name DJs. Being a big name doesn't necessarily mean you're good. They never did it to me though!

PT: *How does it work with the agents?*

AS: You can either go exclusively with a management company or I would recommend when you first start out sign on with as many agencies as possible so they can all get you work. But with some of them it's like modelling – they take on a fee and say they'll get you work but they don't, so be wary of those kinds of people. When you sign up you sign a contract. I would advise not signing a contract when you first start or at least get a lawyer to check it over. When I first signed I was so desperate to get an agent I just signed anything and didn't check it properly and when I wanted to leave because they weren't doing a good job it was a problem. Especially if you do well and you're stuck with them and they're not doing a good job, it can become quite difficult to leave.

PT: *What fee do they take?*

AS: What happens is you join the agency and they take a percentage of your earnings. Some take a percentage of what you've charged and they take that off the promoter as well. So they take 15 per cent off you, 15 per cent of your fee from the promoter or some just charge a straight booking fee from the promoter and a percentage from you. Others just charge a percentage from you or a percentage from the promoters. There's so many different deals out there but it all depends on the DJ and what level you are. I would say the better known you are the better deal you can get. When you first start out the best deal you can get is a percentage. It's normally 10 for an agent, 15 to 20 for management. So when you start out you shouldn't be giving any more than 10 per cent of your fee on an agency level. What they will do is add your name to a roster. If you get on a roster with big DJs then hopefully you get picked. Some agencies have designated people who look after three DJs and they'll push you. They ring round and say we've got this hot new DJ and send out your CD – you've got to have a good CD, don't bother with tapes. They send it out to promoters so you get booked. Some agencies – it shouldn't really happen but it does happen – will say, if you want so and so on the roster then you've got to take so and so. The bigger DJs probably don't know it's happening to them.

PT: *Do a lot of new professional DJs get ripped off?*

AS: Yeah, I got ripped off. I've heard lots of cases of agencies telling you they were charging £100 and they're really charging £300 and not telling you. When you find out further down the line it's very difficult to get that money back so you've got to be quite vigilant. There's sharks out there as in any business.

PT: *Do you need to get an accountant?*

AS: I cannot overemphasise the importance of getting an accountant from day one. When I first started I didn't really think of it as a proper job, no one really advised me to be taking notes of what I was earning. I got investigated by the Inland Revenue and severely fined for not keeping proper records. Get a good accountant because I got an accountant who wasn't chartered and he was the reason I got into trouble. Get one who knows the music business – that's really important. There's been a massive crackdown on DJs. When I went for my interview the investigator actually had newspaper cuttings of interviews I'd done from when I first started in 1994. He had it cut out and in a file. He'd taken notes of posters with my name on and flyers and clippings from *Mixmag* where clubs had mis-advertised me, and I had to prove I hadn't played the gigs. Sometimes you get advertised for clubs where you're not playing – sometimes it's a mistake. The Inland Revenue is vigilant and they are cracking down on DJs big time – they have been for five years.

PT: *I suppose they've heard all the stories about DJs being paid huge amounts.*

AS: Exactly. The tax man had this article and he said, "I hear you get paid £1,000 a gig," and I was being paid nothing like that so I had to prove that I wasn't. All I can say is keep proper books of everything that you do. Even when you start because if your name's on a flyer it's guaranteed someone somewhere at the tax office will have it. Do you know what the worst thing was? The guy that investigated me was actually a clubber that used to come and see me play. He came to my gigs and kept all the flyers from where I played and that was the thing that hurt the most – a clubber betraying me. Awful! It was the worst time of my life and went on for two years. My accountant didn't give me any advice and left me to go to the tax interviews on my own.

PT: *You talked earlier about the dangers of going to a club on your own as a female. Should you take someone with you for security?*

AS: Take a guy or a couple of girls. Don't go on your own. Having said that I think the scene has grown up a lot but you never know, and especially when you're starting out people think they can take advantage of you. It's like being safe whatever you do and wherever you go, especially at night. I used to drive to Manchester every week and I'd be walking out in Manchester at five o'clock in the morning on my own to my car.

PT: *Is press coverage important?*

AS: Being in the press is all-important because promoters do read *Mixmag*, they do read *DJ Magazine* and especially abroad they look to the British press to book their DJs. I started off by ringing the local press. Whenever I had a gig in a town I'd ring the local newspaper and tell them what I was doing. There's no shame in that self-promotion. Trying to get the press on side is really important these days. I was really lucky because the club I played at attracted a lot of press purely because it was a mixed club, they were pro-women and at that time it was a big deal, so there were people in the club taking pictures anyway. Being a girl I was always getting my photo taken, I make no bones about it! That's where image comes into it. I'm not saying you have to be good-looking or glamorous or anything but a strong image just helps and having some presence behind the decks can help attract press and for DJing in general. Look like you're enjoying yourself and the music. Sometimes I feel like shit, I don't want to do the gig but as soon as I put the records on I'm jumping around and people see that and they react to it and it automatically gives everyone a buzz. If you're enjoying it, they're enjoying it. There's nothing worse than seeing a DJ just head down playing his records. It's like, sod off! People want more these days.

PT: *DJs are more like pop acts nowadays.*

AS: Do a few jokes, bring a few props! Yes it's sad but true, you do have to be a more interesting DJ these days to get noticed.

PT: *Is it important to play in Ibiza?*

AS: Ibiza is not what it was but it's quite a good place if you're looking for work to go to because it's quite easy to get warm-up slots because there's so many bars. You won't get paid but it's a good place to get experience. You might get a set in a club and people walking past might like you. If I were starting out now I'd take a bag of records and go to Ibiza. So if you get a job flyering in Ibiza and you happen to take your records, if the DJ doesn't turn up you might get a chance to play. I started out by selling tapes and doing flyering for clubs and by doing that I got to know all the people in all the record shops and promoters in the clubs because I used to sell all their tapes. It is all about getting to know people. It's not what you know it's who you know in the entertainment business. If you send a tape in to a club take it in person and try to get people to remember who you are.

PT: *Is it important to have a good DJ name?*

AS: I hate some DJ names. I like just a name – a name is good like Tim so and so. I like that. All the DJs who have made it big like Lisa Lashes or Carl Cox they're all roll off the tongue kind of names – except maybe Paul Oakenfold. You've got to have sort of a showbiz name but if you're going to change your name don't make it too made up and stupid sounding. Try and make it sound like a credible name. If you're called Jonathan Thistlethwaite you're in trouble!

PT: *Should you have other strings to your bow to make you stand out from the crowd?*

AS: Obviously music production. It's so big now. A great way of getting into DJing is to be producing your own records. Judge Jules can play trumpet for God's sake! Like we were saying, you've got to be more than just head down DJ. I do a bit of TV now – presenting for MTV and BBC. Try to get on the local student radio station and get a show if you can. Music journalism is another thing. I love writing. Plus what I would like to do eventually is pass my knowledge on to someone else – manage and nurture young talent. I'd like to get back into playing the guitar and work that in somehow but I don't know how it would work. You know the way Orbital perform? I think the scene needs something else.

PT: *What other advice do you have?*

AS: Turn up for your set a good half an hour before to listen to what the other DJ is playing and make sure you don't play the same records. These days everyone's got the same records and I think that's why now I play more CDs. I can make a track in the studio that day, burn it onto a CD and no one else will have that, if you're going to get into music production. By the time a track's released now it's guaranteed that all the DJs in your genre will have it.

PT: *What horror stories do you have of DJing?*

AS: A recurring nightmare of mine is I open my record box and there's nothing but Neil Diamond and old Kylie records and all the crowd are slow clapping and I'm late and I can't find my records and I can't make the music work! I turned up to the wrong club once and popped in and put my records on in the DJ box and they were like, "Who the fuck are you?"! One time the DJ before me bent the needle and it would only play the first two inches of any record so I kept having to find records that had two tracks on each side to play more out! I've played at a university gig where the monitors didn't work and you couldn't cue the record properly. Everyone was just standing around on the dancefloor with their arms folded. One thing good management can do for you is check the equipment out before you get there. The best DJ in the world can't mix without a monitor.

PT: *Have you ever made a complete idiot of yourself?*

AS: One time I was playing in this club and they had a sprung dancefloor and I had really high-heeled shoes on. So the decks wouldn't jump they had them suspended from the ceiling from wires and milk crates behind so they had something to steady them on. I lost my balance and I grabbed the decks to steady myself and I swung out and careered off the stage onto the dancefloor but really hurt myself and fell about three feet onto the floor in front of everyone. I ran round and as I was taking my shoes off I knocked the plug out of the socket so all the power went off. The promoters came over and went, "What the fuck are you doing?!"

I was bowled over by the incredible determination and courage of this attractive but slightly built blonde with the pink streak in her hair. In her trendy combat jacket and white pointy shoes she certainly doesn't look like the kind of tough lady who has spent hours beatmatching records to get her mixing right and six years of knock-backs before she had finally made it. What can I say – I was impressed. The idea that you could become a superstar DJ in the spin of a record and make a million overnight was fast being shown up for what it was – a complete fallacy. Success was the culmination of years of hard graft, careful marketing and shrewd promotion with a dollop of the right advice and a side serving of sheer luck. Acting on Anne's advice I also decided that it might not be a bad idea to find out more about music production for my next DJ assignment to add a few extra strings to my fledgling bow.

8

Putting A Track Together

It was one of those truly miserable wet afternoons when every-thing outside looks drab and grey, as though you've woken up to find you're living on the set of *EastEnders*. Tottenham where I lived with Nina had a habit of looking like that most days in the winter anyway and didn't improve all that much in the summer months. My bedroom, which doubled as an office, looked out onto an alleyway where the local kebab shop owners rejoiced in dumping their catering rubbish. In fact to be fair it wasn't just the locals. People came from miles around in the middle of the night merely to tip their old shit in our backyard – anything from used tyres, to burnt out cars and industrial sized freezers. I once sat in horror as a huge pick-up truck arrived and in broad daylight, as bold as brass, fly-tipped its entire load of manure in the alley. Our next-door neighbour once gleefully told us that a few years ago the body of a prostitute had been found abandoned there. It didn't surprise me one iota. Calls to the council were pointless. As soon as one lot of rubbish was cleared new stuff simply appeared out of nowhere. There is obviously some truth in that saying, "nature abhors a vacuum". At least in Haringey.

But I digress. Doug was away on a boys' weekend – no doubt getting up to all sorts (like arguing the pros and cons of Applemac versus PC which was what he and his friends tended to do when they congregated) – and in order to relieve my boredom I'd decided to set aside the afternoon for the embarrassing task of trying to write a music track of some kind. The problem was that I had few ideas and the unhelpful view from my window of calor gas bottles and a burnt out 2CV offered little in the way of musical inspiration. Wyclef Jean might be able to write lyrics about the troubles of 'the projects, man' – what I assumed were the equivalent of our council estates – but as a white middle-class female I would have felt a bit of a fraud.

The previous week I had been to see white female rapper Princess Superstar and she blew me away. Dubbed the female Eminem she had at that time a track in the charts entitled 'Bad Babysitter', which was all about er . . . this rather badly behaved babysitter who had her "boyfriend in the shower" whilst she was meant to be looking after the kid and subsequently tried to get off with the kid's father. Anyhow, I knew it was a daft idea but it planted the crazy seed in my head of – yes you've guessed it – trying to attempt some rapping. After all, I had a few minor qualifications for the task. Besides residing in the ghetto of Tottenham, man, I used to write poems in relatives' birthday cards when I was a kid and I'd written a couple of – albeit appalling – songs in my music class at school. We'd had to write one about a social issue so my group and I chose to do, or rather I imposed the idea of doing, one on the cruelty of keeping animals in zoos. That's how the immortal lines – "How would you like it, kept in a zoo/ people walking round staring at you/ Waking every morning to look through bars/ kept like a specimen in a jar" were penned. Pure Lennon & McCartney genius.

Following the writer's maxim – always write about what you know – I decided to pen something simple about a real-life experience – namely the poor turnout at our club night Refreshment. In homage I composed several dire verses about trying to entice various friends to come down to the club and all of them had different stupid excuses, from ironing boyfriends underpants to DIY, apart from my parents and my granny who turned up to support me. Following in the hiphop tradition of ripping off old records and being a bit of a Gary Numan fan on the quiet, I decided it would be a great idea to try to rap over the intro riff of 'Are Friends Electric?' and then made up a little catchy chorus which I attempted to sing. The problem was my lack of tools for the job. Obviously I had my decks but no recording equipment besides my tiny hand-held Dictaphone that I used for doing interviews at work. I had to keep spinning the record back and recording each verse over the top into my Dictaphone. Aside from the total absence of rapping skills and my strange mixture of Cambridge-educated/Essex vowels, probably reminiscent of the fabled Queen Mother's impersonation of Ali G, the finished product, if cringe-worthy, wasn't actually too bad. I was pretty chuffed with myself, a recording artist at last!

Imagine my dumbfounded horror when whistling, I stepped into the kitchen to make a cup of tea and switching the radio on and – this is the God's honest truth – heard the familiar strains of 'Are Friends Electric?' but with female voices singing over the top. It was one of the first airplays of 'Freak Like Me' by The Sugababes. I didn't know whether to laugh maniacally, cry, or run around the flat making monkey noises whilst sticking my fingers in my ears. Admittedly there was now no market whatsoever for my pathetic little offering (not that one existed anyway) but by the same token I was cheered that bizarrely, despite the fact this was my first ever stab at making a recording, I had somehow hit on a similar formula to this single which went on to be highly successful. It's a very strange world. Suffice it to say that I relayed this strange anecdote to a number of my friends but refused to play any of them the 'underground' Dictaphone recording, no matter how much they begged!

Graeme Park pioneered house music in the UK, playing at the legendary Haçienda nightclub in Manchester no less. He is also an accomplished saxophonist and in collaboration with Paul Burchill from M People produces his own dance music tracks, as well as DJing at Galaxy FM and Renaissance. I asked him for some guidance on starting out in music production. He revealed that now thanks to computer software bedroom DJs everywhere can try making their own dance music tracks.

PT: *How did you become a DJ?*

GP: I got into DJing by accident. About 18 years ago I used to work in a record shop in Nottingham and the guy who owned the shop bought a nightclub and because I was one of his employees he said, "Oh, you're going to DJ at my new club." I said, "Oh dear," but I really enjoyed it and after about a year of doing the record shop and the club I gave up the shop and I've been DJing ever since. So it's not something I ever planned to do, which is often annoying to people. You get lots of young kids coming up in clubs and asking how did you become a DJ and you say that and they go, "Oh, that's not very good is it?"! The thing is that nowadays everyone wants to be a DJ. It's frightening. And so many people *do* DJ as well. They have a weekly job and then at weekends go and DJ. Eighteen years ago when I started it just didn't have the same kudos that it has now. In fact it was seen as a pretty naff job actually. Some people say it still is a naff job to be honest!

PT: *And then you learnt mixing techniques? Were you self-taught?*

GP: Well I play saxophone and I used to play in school orchestras, and before I was a DJ I used to play in bands. So being a musician anyway, just translating that to turntables was quite easy really. I always argue that basic beat mixing is easy but some people make a real hash of it because they think it's this amazing thing, where you see people going, "Oh God, DJs are so clever and DJs are so fantastic," and they're not at all really. Basic beat mixing is really simple. Anyone can learn basic chords on a piano or on a guitar and similarly anyone can learn basic mixing. The hard thing is then within the confines of that doing something original, which I like to think that over the years I've done. That's what being a DJ is all about.

PT: *And do you think it's important to be musical?*

GP: No, it's not but it helps. You've got to have a basic sense of rhythm otherwise you can't do it. You get those people that you see maybe two or three times a year on the dancefloor who don't have any sense of rhythm – I don't think they'd really be able to DJ. The funny thing is they always dance in my line of vision, which is really off-putting! You're DJing and mixing away and you look at everyone and they're all doing the same and one person is completely off. There is an argument that they do have rhythm, it's just that they're at a more advanced level and I quite like that, but it's too advanced when it's in your eye line! It's not important to have a musical background but I think a basic knowledge would help.

PT: *Presumably with music production it doesn't help if you're tone deaf?!*

GP: Well, considering some happy hardcore records out there I'd have to say that was the case! I think again, like creating any music it's down to the individual and what's inside but yeah, you need to know basic things like what works and what doesn't. But with dance music that's less of an issue because it's quite simple to sit down with a computer program like ProTool and just put lots of stuff from other records in there and layer them up to make a new track. A lot of dance music is just samples from records, which is fine but I prefer to go for more creative stuff. I get sent over 100 records a week and you do get lots of stuff that's just lifted from other people's records, from classic old soul or disco records. They're put over a funky kind of tough beat. It works in a club and people like to dance to it but I tend to think, hang on a minute, where's the originality in that? But then some people would argue that it's just a natural extension of what DJs do, which is play other people's records. So to take them and put them onto a record isn't much different.

PT: *It's like recycling.*

GP: Yes it is. It's fine and I play those records and over the years I've been guilty of doing it myself but not over and over again. I much prefer – maybe because I'm getting older – if I've got 10 records that are all sampled stuff and really obvious floor filler records and 10 records that are totally original, all unique, those ones I prefer to play and do try to and I'm quite proud of the fact. Over the past 18 years I've stuck to what I like rather than what I think people want to hear. No matter how big or popular a record is, if I don't like it, if my heart isn't into it I won't play it.

PT: *So you're not one of those DJs that plays to the crowd?*

GP: Yeah I do – you've got to play to the crowd because otherwise if you don't you're going to have an empty dancefloor and also they're not going to come back and see you next time. I think I've always been lucky that people like what I play. But then maybe I've been doing it so long that people have an idea of what I'm about, and also being at the Haçienda and being one of the first people in the country to play house music, that obviously works to my advantage. But you still get people coming up and asking, will you play such and such a record, and I say, "But I haven't got it." And they say, "What do you mean you haven't got it, it's massive," and I say, "Exactly – it's massive and I don't like it." Plus there are some records that you like at first but after a few weeks you're sick of playing this record and you can hear it everywhere you go. So then I take the view that if you can hear that record everywhere and I'm getting a bit sick of it then it's time for me to stop playing it and some people don't understand that either but they're people who want to hear records they know. A lot of up-and-coming DJs, I think they make the mistake of playing those records too much, thinking that that's what's going to make them successful, when in actual fact if you want to be successful you should do your own thing and try to do something no one else is doing.

PT: *Is moving into music production another way that DJs can give themselves an edge?*

GP: Absolutely. Just because you're a good DJ doesn't mean you're going to be good at production and now it works the other way because a lot of people who've made a name for themselves producing great records who then go to start DJing find it difficult. But occasionally it does work. Masters at Work are a great example – Louie Vega and Kenny Gonzales. Great DJs and when you get them in the studio, amazing producers. Others are David Morales and Frankie Knuckles. They're all American though. I'm struggling to think of some British examples. I think all the great DJs who are good at producing tend to be American. I've only just thought of that now!

PT: *How did you yourself get into production?*

GP: If you go right back I used to play in bands and we made demo tapes. We supported quite big acts and I like to think if we'd stuck with it we would have ended up getting signed to a label. So in my mid to late teens I was in recording studios and as a sax player I learnt about miking things up and making my horrible noise sound quite good. But then in 1986 I set up a record label with a guy who owned a recording studio in Derby called Square Dance and that's when Midi was really starting to take over and I learnt about sequencing and that's when the Atari computer started to be the computer for music software and sequencing programs. That's when Cubase appeared.

PT: *So computers have been used for a long time?*

GP: Yeah. When I first started making house music, we had a label called Submission Records, and I used to record under the name 'Groove'. Before we had computers there was a little machine and you had to punch every beat in and if you forgot where you were you had to start again. One day the guy who owned the recording studio came in and said, "Right we're going to do it through this Atari computer." Then suddenly you could see everything on the screen and see exactly how you were building the song. That's just developed to such a point now that Macintoshes are the industry standard computers. Cubase is still used but ProTool is just a lot more versatile for editing sound waves and audio. Also for working on radio Protool is very useful for doing speech. I remember when I first started in the studio if you did a really good club record and it was six and a half minutes long and then someone said, "Right we need a radio edit," what you had to do was get a razor blade and your tape and cut the bits out and edit it down that way.

Now it's all done on computer. You can hide your edits as well. With a piece of tape you cut it and you join this bit to this bit but if there's a crash cymbal that suddenly stops where you cut it, it sounds awful. But if you've got a computer you can cut this bit out, join these bits together but then you can fade them into each other so your crash cymbal still crashes and fades away. You can do really basic editing on minidiscs too, because again with a minidisc you can chop things up and you can move the bit you've chopped out to the end of the minidisc and if you make a mistake and it doesn't quite work you can put it back in again. The technology that exists is just amazing. Dance music is so easy to make. Cubase most bedroom DJs would have.

PT: *So there are bedroom DJs out there making music?*

GP: You can get really carried away. Cubase has got all these virtual instruments in it. It's got lots of old classic analogue synths, old Hammond organs. That's what I do at home. I work with a guy called Paul Burchill who used to play with M People and he's got a proper little studio. But at home I can put basic ideas into Cubase. I've got a keyboard and a computer and I put basic ideas into Cubase, then export the Cubase stuff to ProTool because it's a bit more versatile. Then I take a CD to Burchy's place and he loads it into his ProTool and with his proper studio he can then make it sound better. Make it sound more fancy, as he keeps saying! But this digital technology is just unbelievable. Even up to as recent as five years ago you needed quite a big sampler with lots of memory and the computer would drive the sampler and if you didn't have enough memory that was it, you couldn't do anymore. But now with ProTool you don't need a sampler because you can record straight into ProTool and mess about that way.

PT: *When you sit down to make a track, where do you start?*

GP: Me and Burchy, when we do stuff as the Park and Burch project, the first thing we start with is a basic drum track and if we're doing a housey thing we'll probably go 127 beats per minute. A basic fall to the floor simple groove and then either one of us will have an idea for a keyboard riff. I tend to come up with a simple bass line and then Burchy, being an incredibly accomplished musician, will with my basic drum track and bass line then come up with some fancy chords and some really good keyboard stuff. Then that will go off in one direction and then we'll go back and change the bass line to match what he's done. The new bass line might make what he's done not relevant anymore and we change it again. Then we'll start to write some lyrics or come up with a melody and then we get these two girls we use to start singing and then it gets to the stage when it really starts to take shape and the original drum track sounds really naff because it sounds basic. That's when I sit down with a load of drum sounds and programme up a complex drum track or if we're a bit pushed for time just sample a couple of drum parts, a couple of bars of stuff and loop it up. I do prefer to create my own drum tracks but then you don't have to, if you just want to use a sampled loop you can. That's fine if you just want to do something that does the job but if you want to go and produce something properly you sit down with something for days and just get the right kickdrum, the right snare drum, the right fills, the right patterns. It's good – you can get really into it. You can get lost in it.

PT: *On average how long does it take you to make a track?*

GP: Last summer when we were really on fire we were doing one really good track a week. But our week would be Monday,

Tuesday and Wednesday about midday to eight o'clock. Working non-stop. The good thing about me and Burchy is we can take it in turns. He can spend two hours doing stuff and I'm just lying on the settee just listening, nodding my head and reading a magazine going, "Yeah, that's wicked," but then he'll go, "I've had enough of this, my head hurts," and I'll go, "Right, off you go," and he will go onto the settee and I'll sit at the computer and mess about with what he's done. It's quite a good working relationship. I can do stuff on my own but it's a lot more basic. While I'm a musician, when it comes to keyboards I'm one hand and Burchy is the full 10 fingers. That's because I'm a saxophonist. With saxophones or any wood instrument you can only play one note at a time, so that translates to how I play the keyboards. I'm good with doing riffs but the good thing about a computer is I can do a chord, record it, play it back and while it's playing do another chord, so I can layer it up to make myself sound like a proper keyboard player. The other thing about working on your own is you can get so bogged down in something that when someone hears it they go, "Mmm yes it's alright," and you go, "But I've just spent days on it!" But if you're working with someone – not anyone, it's got to be someone you get on with, someone you have a mutual respect for and preferably the same bizarre sense of humour – then together you can accomplish something much better and hopefully not something self-indulgent. There's nothing worse than that. I think you need someone to feed off.

PT: *So you don't disappear up your own bottom?*

GP: Yes. Another thing that me and Burchy do, because Burchy knows a lot of jazz musicians and he's got a northern soul band as well, we'll work on a track and then when we go back to it a few weeks later we'll go, "Wow that bass would sound great if it was played by a real bass player." Burchy picks up the phone. The next day this guy comes and does this funky proper bass and it sounds much better now. But because you've got a real bass what we need now is some jazz guitars. So Burchy picks up the phone, a guy comes down and does jazz guitar the next day. I really like translating things, electronic stuff that we've done into real musicians and although digital technology has improved to such a level now that your average punter might not be able to distinguish between real or digital copies, as soon as you have a real musician in the warmth just takes over. There's no substitute for a real bass line and a real guitar. In the old days you'd have to spend hours if not days trying to make sure everything was perfect but now you can pay the bass player for two hours, off he goes, then you can sit down and take everything that he's done and mess about with it and repeat it and it still sounds real but it's just been tweaked a little bit.

PT: *Since records were first invented people have been worrying that live musicians might become obsolete.*

GP: No. Never. There's been a real revival, a real surge in percussionists in clubland and dance music because any basic software program has got basic percussion sounds and you can just do old conga riffs, but then you get a real percussionist in the studio, even if you're only going to sample a little bit of it and use that one little bit over and over again, still the sound and the fact it's a real person doing it gives it more energy. You can sit there programming congas and then put a groove on to try and push it across the beat and it'll sound good, but get the real human being in and oh, there's no substitute for it. Strings are the only thing I haven't translated into electronic copies. Strings never sound quite right. To get a full string section is prohibitively expensive but luckily Burchy knows so many different violin players and cello players.

PT: *How much does it cost to hire session musicians?*

GP: You've got your basic Musicians Union flat rates – I should know because I'm a member. Not a great deal. But even if you wanted a six-piece string section, that's six people you've got to pay an hourly rate and they've got to set up and it's just getting the space. I mean, Burchy's using a small place. But the way around that is if you know someone who plays violin and someone who plays cello then hopefully the violin player will have several violins or a viola and you can do one piece and then play it back and add a harmony, then another one and before you know it you've got what sounds like a six-piece string section.

PT: *So it's just thinking in a flexible way?*

GP: Exactly. When we do brass it's just me on my own with my alto saxophone and my tenor saxophone. It helps if you get a trumpet in there too.

PT: *What do you think makes a successful track or a good track?*

GP: A successful track is something everyone likes. Some records just arrive through my door, you put it on and think wow, this is going to be massive. But a successful record isn't necessarily a good record though. Popular doesn't necessarily mean good – you've only got to look at the charts over the last

50 years to see that. But at the end of the day it's all down to personal taste. Some records I absolutely love but people just don't see it. Similarly, there's a lot of records that are absolutely massive but I just refuse to play because I hate them. It's a very personal thing really.

PT: *There's records that always get people on the dancefloor.*

GP: Yeah, those common denominator records. Stuff that captures the moment but then, if you go back to them two or three years later, some of them sound awful. I like to stick to records that hopefully sound good in years to come. With Burchy and me our stuff comes from the heart. We could sit down and do one of those common denominator records but our hearts wouldn't be in it. There's a lot of cynicism in the dance music industry at the moment. People just doing things for the sake of it, making a record because they think it will be a big record. That's just my view but I get a lot of stuff sent to me every week and a lot of it is rubbish. Independent labels are where all the quality stuff comes from.

PT: *How do you get your track from the bedroom to being released by a record label?*

GP: There was a time when you'd have to take your record to loads of record companies and hope that somebody would like it and put it out. But now what you do is you burn it onto a CD and you give it to a DJ who plays it in a club and everyone goes mental, you're very happy and you then go and press up 1,000 white labels and you make certain key record stores get those white labels and make sure other key DJs get the record. If the DJs play it people want to buy it, so they buy it from the record

141

shop and before you know it there's 1,000 white labels out there and the record's doing pretty well but nobody can get it because they've all been sold out. So then you either take the plunge and press some more or go to a record company, it doesn't have to be a major – one of the independents – and they'll put it out for you. That's the ideal scenario really but you can go into the studio in the morning and by six o'clock in the next morning after a heavy night you burn your CD and take it to a club night and try it out and then you can see straight away, wow this really is rubbish! Or, yeah this really works and then you can go back to the studio and play with it a bit more. That's the thing – it's so instant. The old days of doing a wonderfully produced track, spending thousands of pounds on it, spending days on it, then getting it rejected by a major record label – those days are gone. You could put a single out – 1,000 white labels – counting everything like making the track for £1,500. Twelve inches sell for about £8 and if you only make £3 after everything else that's £3,000, which you then put into another one. Everyone should set up their own record label. In fact, I've just thought, why haven't I set up mine? Actually I used to and it was a nightmare!

Wow. I had no idea making music could be so simple. I'd thought in my ignorance I'd have to shell out thousands of pounds on building a studio or at least hiring one to make music properly, whereas all I needed to do was go out and buy myself some software. There were probably thousands of bedroom DJs out there doing just that and getting their tracks pressed onto those mysterious white labels. I was already the proud owner of one myself – having bought it purely by accident in a record shop because I'd mistaken it for something else. My friend Alastair had admired it sitting in my record bag and I pretended I'd bought it knowing it was some cool 'underground' thing.

Now I too could put my own one out – that is, if I could come up with something better than my first offering, already scuppered by The Sugababes. I'd have to put my creative cap on – although I was pretty certain I'd give the white Essex girl rapper a miss this time.

9

DJ Masterclass

Following my premature foray into music production my thoughts returned to my fledgling DJing skills. They were coming along now thanks to a bit of practice but there was still something missing. Suffice it to say that there are DJs and there are DJs but what I wanted to know was what is that essence that sets the great and good apart from the also-rans? I was still a humble L-plated turntablist and might never achieve the pinnacle of mediocrity let alone success but I was more than a little curious to find out what DJs considered to mark out the likes of Roger Sanchez – whose name kept cropping up in conversations with my interviewees as the DJ's DJ – from their jobbing peers.

I scoured the DJ community far and wide gleaning gems of advice and tips – from the Dave Pearce of Radio 1 to the great Sanchez himself – and these are to be found at the end of this chapter.

But firstly I sought the masterclass advice of DJ Les Adams who runs one of the country's most prestigious DJ courses at the Academy of Contemporary Music in Guildford. The course is full-time, lasts two years and teaches students everything there is to know about DJing many types of music as well as how to handle themselves successfully on the business side. Back in the Nineties Les beat Brandon Block and Tall Paul to take the crown of DJ Of The Year. The first DJ to enter the UK charts in his own right as LA Mix, Les was a prolific remixer and music producer, remixing many artists from Aretha Franklin to Cameo and has produced Danni Minogue. He lectures at ACM during the day and amazingly still finds the time to DJ six nights a week.

PT: *How did you become a DJ?*

LA: I'm an accidental DJ. I ran a mobile disco with my brother when I was 14 or 15. Then when I was working in a hi-fi shop it opened up a professional audio division selling DJ equipment and we did an installation in a West End club called Napoleon's. It was a gay club and I was invited along to the opening night. The owner wanted me there because it was one of the best sound systems in London. He wanted me there to make sure everything worked and the DJ who was supposed to do the opening night had a car accident and didn't turn up. It wasn't serious – he wasn't hurt but his car was. So I was the only person who knew how to use the equipment and had any kind of DJing experience and I ended up DJing for a few hours. And then the DJ arrived and we got chatting and I started DJing on his nights off. I was into all the music – it was Hi-NRG dance music – and I ended up as a resident DJ. I was doing both jobs to start with – working day and night. Hi-fi shop during the day and this club at night. And then I was spotted by one of the managers who worked at Regine's nightclub in Kensington – it's now called the Roof Garden and at the time was the top nightclub in London. Anyone who turned down a job working at Regine's was mad. So I was offered the residency but I was still doing both jobs and very tired all the time and one morning driving to my day job I had a car accident – fell asleep at the wheel and this forced me into making a decision that I had to do one or the other. So I decided to give up my day job and became a DJ.

PT: *So how did you get into remixing?*

LA: I was driving home from the club one night and listening to Radio Luxembourg – and on there was a DJ called Tony Prince and he had a show called the DJ Mix Express and he had just started DMC (Dance Mix Club). And at that time the members received a cassette tape each month with mixes on and he was playing these on his radio show. Tony asked the DJs listening if they wanted to send in a mix tape, so I put something together and posted it to him and he phoned me up. He did his show from London and sent it out to Luxembourg. So he invited me to his home – DMC was being run from a room in his house – and said, "Can you do some mixes for the show." As DMC grew so did my reputation and the record industry started taking notice of what I was doing. I got a call one day from the A&R man for Club Records and they had Cameo signed to them and he said, "I love the stuff you've been doing, I'd like you to do a megamix of Cameo tracks. We've got this song on the album called WordUp – it's not very good, see what you can do with it." So suddenly here I am in a recording studio, remixing a track for Cameo and this is surreal! How did this happen to me, I'm a DJ! They loved the remix and it went to number one in the dance charts and then it was like, Les Adams is the man to do remixes and I ended up doing Tina Turner, Aretha Franklin, Grace Jones. At that time – mid- to late-Eighties – there was a real fashion for megamixes. Every artist who had more than two records out had to have a megamix and I did most of them.

I left Regine's, in fact I walked out one Saturday night. The club hostess had a boyfriend in America who was a DJ and she wanted him to come and work there and she put the pressure on. One night I just had enough. I left a record playing on the turntable at one o'clock in the morning on a Saturday night and I got up and as I walked past the checkout desk she was standing there and I said to her, "You have got precisely three minutes to find another DJ because that record that's playing is the last one and it's going to run out and I'm going home." And that was it. Two days later I got a letter sacking me but by then I'd moved on to bigger and better things anyway. I've earned a living at it ever since. I still DJ six nights a week now – I've got a gig tonight.

PT: *So what's the secret?*

LA: Over the years I suppose the secret of staying in this industry and actually making a career out of it is to keep up to date with the music and to be prepared to adapt to new styles. In the late Seventies I was playing Hi-NRG disco, early Eighties I'm playing jazz funk and soul – that continued really through the Eighties and then I got into more commercial dance music. And since then I've had a bandanna round my head and played acid house and hard house. Up until six months ago I had so many different gigs each week playing different styles of music. In London I was doing a Wednesday night at Eros in Enfield, on a Friday night in Destiny at Watford – both those nights I'm playing UK garage and got a reputation in London as a garage DJ. Sunday night I used to fly up to Glasgow and play hard house in a club and there they knew me as a techno DJ. Somewhere over Manchester flying I turn from a garage DJ into a hard house DJ. But now I'm playing at places like Brannigans where I'm playing party music – I play a bit of Abba, 'Ice Ice Baby' and all those cheesy tunes and then on Sunday I do a set where I play pure R&B. Now, having all those different styles means that I'm working six nights a week and I always have – I've never been out of work as a DJ.

PT: *So do you still* enjoy *these different styles, or are you ever in a club and you think, God I really hate this?*

LA: I got to the stage with garage that I really wasn't enjoying what I was playing. The problem with UK garage music at the moment is it's all gone very underground and very dark. It's all big bass lines and MCs and that kind of stuff doesn't work now in the commercial venues.

PT: *Then there's the guns, etc . . .*

LA: Exactly. There's all the violence that goes along with it and everybody's an MC and they want to have a go on the mic. That's not really what I want to do. And I found that I was playing the same music that I'd been playing for months. There was just no new music coming through that was commercial or accessible enough for the dancefloors I was playing to. And the people were still into garage but they only liked the old stuff. So in the end I left Watford and now I play commercial dance and R&B. But I do enjoy it – I particularly like R&B at the moment – there's a lot of very, very good records out there and I'm pleased that R&B is there because otherwise I don't know what I'd be playing at the moment. Probably house, but even a lot of that is going very underground. A particular DJ hero of mine is Roger Sanchez and I went to see him play at Turnmills recently, in fact I was employed by Pioneer – because he's sponsored by Pioneer – and I was asked by them to go along. How good is this, I was paid to go along to Turnmills, stand in the DJ box with Roger Sanchez, drinking champagne – and it's tough enough to get into the place. I loved the music he was playing but it's not music that I have a sufficient knowledge of that I would feel happy enough to go out and do a set. I've always tried to stay on the commercial edge of things because as soon as you start to specialise in something you get pigeonholed. I did get to the stage in London where the company I was working for were not offering me gigs doing commercial dance because they'd written me off as a garage DJ, whereas I'm quite happy to stand and play anything. I think my criteria for being a DJ has changed. It used to be for the music. Now I still love the music but the thing that I do it for now, apart from the money, is the buzz that you get from the crowd.

PT: *So you still get the buzz?*

LA: Yeah. When you do a good mix and you just drop the bass line in right and you've got the next tune on and you get a scream from the dancefloor it still sends shivers up my spine. And that feeling has never gone. If the day comes when I don't get that feeling anymore it will be time for me to give up. At my age – which incidentally is a national secret – I'm playing to audiences but a lot of them are young enough to be my children. In fact some of them probably are! Let me meet your mother and I'll tell her if I remember! But at the same time because I keep myself very up to date with the music it's very rare to catch me out with a tune, providing what you're asking for is something that's on the commercial side of the genre. So keeping on top of the music and just being able to relate to the audience is important. I know a lot of DJs who started out when I did who are now doing other jobs purely because they are now saying, "Yeah, well, today's music is rubbish," and they haven't moved with the times.

PT: *What's the philosophy behind the course you run because most of the people I've spoken to have learnt from their friends at home?*

LA: DJing has had a raw deal as far as image is concerned over the years. The point of the ACM course is it recognises DJing as a profession. Years ago it was, yeah you're a DJ but what do you do for a living? DJing was something you did at the weekend. But the ACM course covers so many different aspects – how to mix, business studies, technology. The people who come on my course by the time they leave know how a CD player works let alone how to use it, they actually know how the laser inside reads the disk. They get some technical knowledge so that when they go to a gig they have a working knowledge of the equipment. I teach them how to set a turntable up properly – so many professional DJs out there just don't know how to balance the arm correctly. The ACM course is really saying this is a career – you can make a living at this. If you're good at it you can make lots of money. I've got friends who've got proper jobs. I've got a friend who's a nurse – that's a proper job but how many hours a week does she work and how much does she get paid? And if that's a proper job I'll stick to this one.

At the end of an ACM course the students will leave with a knowledge of everything. There's a whole lecture that's coming up in a few weeks time that is about relationships. It's important for a DJ to have good relationships with managers in clubs. How to talk to promoters, how to conduct yourself in business. Instead of going along on a gig and saying, "Well, I'm a DJ, give me a job – I've got my bag of records and I'm better than this bloke you've got on now" – which is the old approach of trying to get a job – with the ACM qualification you can actually say I've trained at the ACM, here's my certificate. The course gives people practical experience as well. We have people playing at Gatecrasher. One of our former students plays at Turnmills and there are these doors and opportunities that open with the backing of the educational authority. It is pushing DJing into almost an area of respectability and that's something DJs haven't had. We're all supposed to be shagging everything that moves and getting drunk.

PT: *What avenues are open to DJs?*

LA: There's so many different areas – radio DJing, club DJing, the DJ is the centre of the musical universe. Without DJs who would play the records on the radio? Who would play them in the clubs, who would listen to them if there weren't DJs? It's also a great area to springboard into other things you want to do if you're a DJ and you conduct yourself properly. You start to form relationships with record companies. They're selling you records, you're giving them reactions and liaising with them and it may be that one day you decide that you want to work in the record industry. That avenue is open to you from being a DJ. If you want to go into music production your knowledge of music and knowing what works on a dancefloor gives you the aware-ness to be able to go into a studio even if you can't play yourself. I've been on *Top Of The Pops* three times – I've had national hits. I was signed to A&M records as an artist, but I can't play a note and I can't sing! But what I did was, I surrounded myself with people who could and produced. So I was actually the pro-ducer and I had people like Juliet Roberts singing on my tracks, top session musicians and we made tunes. My biggest hit got to number three in the national chart. I've had five number one dance hits, six records in the Top 40 – see the gold discs around the room. I've produced Danni Minogue – tracks on her *Love And Kisses* album and all from the springboard of being a DJ.

PT: *You're still into the music and have a lot of energy but I imagine there must still be a time limit on the job and you must think, what will I do after it's all over.*

LA: You do have to keep an eye on the future. As I get older I think to myself I can't do this forever. But at the moment I'm still working six nights a week and if I do want to move on I don't have a problem, I can still find the gigs. But the area I'd like to move into more is the lecturing and the educational side of things. You have to make a plan and think about what you want to be doing when you're 50. At 18 or 20 you don't need to be planning much yet but certainly by the time you reach 25 you can't just go around thinking it's going to last forever. It lasts longer for some than others and, as we said, it depends on your taste in music.

PT: *So what do you think really marks out the successful DJs from the also-rans?*

LA: I don't know what makes a DJ successful because I think there are certain successful DJs out there who actually are not very good.

PT: *You mean they haven't done your course?!*

LA: It's not even that! There are certain people working out there who are based largely on image. I can tell you why certain DJs are better than others. The likes of Roger Sanchez – when I watch him work I don't know whether it's just that he's got such great ears for picking good music but the way he mixes it together he almost knows what the crowd want before they do. He can read it and you know when he mixes in the next tune that the crowd are going to love it. You don't go along thinking that the next tune might not be as good as this one. He always delivers and I think a sign of a really good DJ is that they know what to play. They know what the crowd like and the timing of their mixing is impeccable.

PT: *How do you teach your students to mix?*

LA: When I'm teaching the ACM students we have a beat and

bar structure that we teach and the ones that mix very well are the ones who follow this structure. A lot of DJs forget that it's not just about synchronising two beats – music is written in a structure. It's a 4/4 rhythm, there are four beats to the bar and everything goes in four bar phrases or multiples thereof. And when you're mixing two records together instead of thinking about it as just mixing two beats, one over the other, what you've actually got is two completely separate groups of musicians recorded in different studios in different parts of the world probably, and what you're trying to make them do is all play together in time.

PT: *Impossible!*

LA: Yeah! They are playing to a structure – music is written in a structure and unless you mix using the same structure as they used when they made the record, timing will be out, things will happen when they shouldn't, vocals will suddenly come in when they shouldn't, bass lines will clash. We teach a notation system that you actually put on the record sleeve and we teach the DJs to analyse every record to work out how many beats there are in the intro, what those beats consist of, whether they're purely percussion which means they have no musical key. Whether there's a bass line which could clash with another bass line and to mark on their record sleeves all this information so when they take a record out to mix it they can look at the notes on the record they're playing, look at the one they're going to mix in and the notes actually tell you how to do the mix and time it perfectly so the bass line always comes in in the right place and that the timing is good. There's also a lot of emphasis on getting the technical side of DJing right. You can do a great mix but if your levels aren't right and this track comes in too loud or too quiet it can destroy the feel and the impact of the mix. There's nothing worse than a DJ mixing into a tune and when he brings the crossfader across the volume goes down and then the energy is lost. Or if it goes up and everyone goes, "What happened there?"

PT: *I have this LTJ Bukem record that I play in a set with my Seventies funk records but I always forget that it's much louder than the others and it comes on and goes "WWAAAAHHH!" and makes everyone jump.*

LA: That's not understanding gain controls and how to set the mixer up properly before you mix into the tune, because you can mix old and new tunes together providing you EQ them right and get the levels right. There'll generally be a difference because of the production techniques used so you never get it absolutely smooth but there are ways and means of getting it right.

PT: *What other skills do you teach?*

LA: One thing that's very important is teaching them to be organised. To keep all your records in BPM order is so important. If you've got five boxes of records in front of you and you're playing a record that is 130 BPM all the tunes that are 110, 115 or 150, 170 are not going to mix with the one you're playing if you try between now and doomsday. And if all your records are mixed up you're looking at things you couldn't possibly play. So by keeping them in BPM order if you're playing a record that is 130 BPM and that's in box four you only need look either side of it. Because either side of that, down to about 126 up to about 134, 135 – these are the only records that are likely to mix with the one you're playing. Then you can make a choice about which is the right one to play. You see DJs hunting through their boxes and what can happen, especially when you've got other distractions like people shouting at you to do a shout for their mate or play this tune, play that tune, you can find yourself running out of time. And you pick the wrong record because you haven't had time to look.

Also, keeping your mind open when you're buying records. Don't just buy the tunes you need now. You might well be playing R&B because that's big. But if there's a few big house tunes out there as well, even if you're not playing house still buy them. Have them in your box because maybe in six months' time you might be asked to do a house gig and invariably you will get requests for people's favourites that might be six months old but if you didn't buy them at the time, you can't buy them now. Try buying records six months after they've gone, three months after they've gone. You can't get them. I buy every-thing – even stuff that's in the charts. I've got the latest Kylie record. I haven't played it yet but if the time comes and I'm doing a party and they want it, it's there.

PT: *What do you teach your students about how to handle themselves with promoters?*

LA: It's a big industry but it's got a very big grapevine. It's the basic rules of being a human being. Treat people as you would like to be treated and even if somebody is a bit of an arsehole to you just retain your dignity and don't give them an excuse to be able to call you arrogant. I won't mention any names but I know two or three DJs who are very good DJs but they have a real attitude problem. They think they're the greatest thing that ever walked God's earth and they can't understand why they're not working six nights a week. They're not working because people don't actually like them as people. They're arrogant, they're pushy. You've got to be pushy to a certain extent to get on but there's a line between being determined and being arrogant and if you fall out with a club manager for any reason, if he comes up and says your set was rubbish or whatever, to argue back and to tell the manager he's a wanker might give you a bit of personal satisfaction at the time but that wanker one day might turn up as your regional manager in a chain of clubs and you ain't ever gonna work any of them. Be nice to people on your way up because you never know when you're going to need them in the future.

There are certain people who if I won the National Lottery and had so much money that I could afford just to retire I'd like to go and punch on the nose. There really are. But right now they're people who might have an affect on my career and whilst I wouldn't condone being two-faced you can be polite, then they'll know you don't like them but never give them the opportunity to say, "Oh Les Adams, he was rude to me." No one will ever say I've been rude to them but that doesn't mean to say I like everyone I've worked with. It's maintaining an air of professionalism. At the end of the day these people pay my wages and people have got to like you to book you. I've done gigs where at the end of the night I've gone, "Oh God that was terrible, I never want to play there again." It happens to everyone, it doesn't matter who you are. I'm sure Sanchez has done gigs in his career where he's walked out thinking, "Christ that was terrible," either his own performance or the crowd weren't on the same vibe but you don't be arrogant about it and you don't let everybody know how upset you are, you just get on with it.

PT: *There's the whole drug culture associated with house music. Are DJs affected by this? Are there DJs who abuse drugs?*

LA: Yes. Not me. I can actually put my hand on my heart and

say that I have never taken any tablets or pills in my life and incredibly, whether this is just the way I come over to people – bearing in mind the number of clubs I've worked in over the years – I've never been offered any. Now I find that quite amazing. In all these different clubs and Scottish house gigs – banging house – nobody's ever come up to me and offered me a pill. A few times in my career I've probably had a few too many drinks and I'm not saying that as, yeah I do it all the time. A couple of times someone buys me a drink and I have one too many and feel a bit light-headed but as soon as I get that feeling I think, enough. I don't like it – I like to feel in control. But there are DJs – again no names – one in particular who's actually a very well-known DJ – and he has said to me he really believes that when he's drunk and done a few pills he mixes better. Only to himself. He thinks he's mixing better because he's out of his head and he's not hearing the double beats, he's not hearing the key clashes because he's so high. Now anybody listening to him would say, really you shouldn't be doing that because you actually play better when you're straight. But there's a lot of drugs going on in DJing and there are those who profess that they play better – and maybe it does open their senses – but from personal experience I've never met any DJs of whom I've thought, yeah he really plays better when he's off his head. So much of mixing is in the coordination and what do drugs do, they mess it all up. How could anybody argue that being on drugs improves your coordination? It doesn't, not from what I've seen! People fall over and they get very silly!

PT: *How do you teach your students to rescue a bad night?*

LA: When they go to a gig they've got to be prepared for all eventualities. If they're booked to play a hard house gig, don't just take hard house records, take a few classics with you. Take

'Let Me Be Your Fantasy' by Baby D. It doesn't matter if the gig turns out to be a hard house gig and you play your hard house tunes and you don't play the classics, that's fine. But what happens if you turn up and halfway through the night it all falls a bit flat. We train them to take what we call bankers. Records you can bank on. Records you know that if you play that record people will dance to it. Two of the biggest commercial bankers of all time 'Show Me Love' by Robin S., 'Make The World Go Round' by Mandy B. with that great bass line.

I remember one night I was at the Ministry of Sound, this was some years ago when it was really good, it's a bit touristy now, and the night was going fairly well but it was getting a little bit moody. People were dancing but they weren't really smiling, they weren't looking like they were having a great time and whoever it was played a blinder because suddenly in the middle of his set he just chopped into 'Where Love Lives' by Alison Limerick. That piano came in and the whole room, the atmosphere lifted and from then on he had them in the palm of his hand and it was just by picking a tune that is going to turn it around. It's important to always carry those records around in your box. Alison Limerick is always in my box – I might only play it twice a year but it's always there. And the other thing is not to panic. If it starts to go wrong try and pull it back. I think what a lot of inexperienced DJs try and do is if they're doing the warm-up set they try too hard to get people dancing. They play too many big records too early and then leave themselves with nothing to play later. What you've got to remember is when you're doing a warm-up set in a club what do you do when you first arrive at a club? Do you get on the dancefloor and dance? No, you go to the bar and have a drink. Are you allowed to take drinks on the dancefloor? No. So once you've bought a drink, even if they play the best tune in the world, you can't go on the dancefloor. People meet their friends there. They don't all arrive at the same time so some people arrive and they have a drink and two minutes later their friends arrive and get a drink. I play this gig once a week and between 10 and 11 I don't try in the slightest to get people up and dancing. I just play music that's familiar, new tunes and I will wait until the club is almost half full before I will put on a big tune and get people dancing. Once you've got the dancefloor going, then you start thinking seriously will this record work, will that record work.

Don't just look at the dancefloor. Look round the edges, look at the bars, see if everybody's happy, see if they're all enjoying what you're playing. Because they're there to be entertained as well – it's not just the people who want to dance. You can sometimes get that enough people are into a certain kind of music, like I'm doing an R&B set and the dancefloor's full of people dancing to R&B, but if the people outside aren't happy I think, well we'll have a change round in a minute and all these people who like R&B can go and we'll get the house people on the dancefloor and you do get this changeover as you change the styles. It's about not panicking and knowing you've got records in reserve, that if all else fails these will work but you only get to know what these records are when you've been a regular clubber and you've seen other DJs play them or if you've been doing it for a while.

Les' coaching was highly insightful. To complement his sage words I searched among the DJing community for further masterclass tips, advice and hints from their wealth of experience.

TIPS FROM THE DJ MASTERS

"Keep practising. Keep fucking up, but keep practising."

Sister Bliss, Faithless

"Protect your neighbours' hearing. Egg cartons stuck to the walls of your bedroom make great DIY soundproofing."

Tony Prince, DMC Chairman

"A friend of mine was a DJ when I was 13 and I was a break dancer. I always wanted to do something a bit different and not just be one of the people in the crowd but be in front of the crowd so I got behind the decks. What helped me become a success was that I started doing my own events and having a record helped bring it all to a different level. I got to be a bit of a self-promoter. You've got to do it yourself. Part of it is losing money at the very beginning. You've got to lose a bit of money to make it worth your while. A successful DJ is a person who is able to communicate and understand the crowd he plays to. It's about psychology. It's making the transition from trying something exciting in the bedroom to moving a crowd. Understanding what they want and having the ability to place yourself on the floor while you're playing. A lot of people get caught in playing big records but anyone can do that. My best advice is find your musical vibe – play from the heart – but be open to different music and be open to different people. Many DJs forget they have a crowd altogether while others play to the crowd too much.

"With promoters, you have to be intelligent about things, don't believe everything you hear. Make it clear when you make a deal at the beginning because if you don't arguments will happen. When you start out and have no management don't sell yourself too short or too high. You have to be able to accommodate people – again it's about psychology. You have to learn the hard way. I definitely learnt the hard way.

"As for the music, part of it is that you have to walk a fine line between being current and sticking to your vibe. People are afraid to move forward at all. DJs suffer from pigeonholing themselves. I tend to find music I love – I don't focus on what's cool, the big hype or a scene and there is a lot of crap around although there's a lot of good music around too.

"You've got to be hungry. It's my 24th year in DJing and I love it now more than ever. I hunt for music constantly and you have to if you want to hear the new music. I talk to a lot of producers and vibes musically to try to get a different sound."

On Ibiza: "This is an island – people come here to get away and it's more conducive to music than being in a big city. It's not an easier place to play but if you know your crowd they're more receptive. The environment is more conducive.

"There's tons of pitfalls in DJing. I'm very much against drugs and people can fall into them easily. There are also a lot of leery promoters out there who just don't do the right thing. Plus beware of yourself – have some quality control and don't be greedy and do ten gigs in a row. Pace is very important and the dangers of a lack of patience hold true, especially when you're building a set. If the crowd doesn't react immediately some DJs panic and play all their big tunes but an hour later they've got nothing left. The impression is that it's an easy way to get money and women but unfortunately it doesn't come as easy as that. You have to have a true love for the music."

Roger Sanchez, Galaxy FM DJ

"I started DJing by just sitting by the stereo and playing records for me and my friends. My career took off after I played at the Paradise Garage which never would have happened without the help of my partner Judy Weinstein who was at the time very connected with the Garage. I also got to meet many great remixers at that time, Shep Pettibone, Steve Thompson, Bruce Forest, Larry Levan and Francois K.

"A successful DJ is one that wants to have fun and entertain the audience. Always pay attention to your audience as well but also be creative. It is about the music, the feeling that you bring. Technique helps but it doesn't mean anything if there is no substance to the music. As far as promoting yourself, well there's several ways. You can try and throw your own parties, make your own records and always remember where you come from no matter how big you get. Avoid shady promoters, bullshit wannabe managers/agents and heavy partying. An important lesson I've learnt along the way is that there's ups and downs during a career and also to leave on time for the airport!"

David Morales, Galaxy FM

"The most important thing for me as a DJ is you have to love the music you are playing, otherwise it's just a technical exercise and you will never be able to take people on a journey or understand the power of the reaction that certain songs can provoke. In terms of the technical aspect I prefer Technics turntables (which are usually fine second-hand and most mixers do the trick). It's all about practising and thinking about what your style is going to be. Go and watch other DJs work, you could be the best bedroom mixer in the world but a floor clearing DJ. Learn to read the audience, are they tired or do they need an energy rush? For me it's all about having a very close bond between the clubbers and the DJ. Above all enjoy it and be prepared for lots of knock-backs on the way."

Dave Pearce – Radio 1

"Via my website I receive at least 25 e-mails a week from people asking how they can get their first gig, and the first thing I tell them is to be patient. There's hardly a DJ out there who earned more from DJing within their first five years than they spent on records. It's essential that you're in it for the long-haul, 'cos nothing's likely to materialise overnight. Nevertheless if you're patient and prepared to generate your own luck by making records, promoting parties, and generally hanging out with others in the industry, you'll end up with a job so satisfactory that it simply doesn't feel like a job. And you can't get much better than that."

Judge Jules

"Like most people of my age I got into DJing because of a love for music – a passion for it and not being good at dealing with social occasions. You can say more with music sometimes than what you say with your mouth so that's how I got into music. At the time electro was breaking through and hiphop and stuff – it was about '82, '83 when I first started DJing and I just really got into it. I did other jobs – I was a civil servant and stuff like that but I didn't really like it and always DJed for other people. It's always been a passion and if you're lucky enough to follow your passion and actually see it all the way through then your work side is always really rewarding. I'd say always follow your heart and if your heart is saying one thing and your head is saying something else listen to your heart when it concerns music. It's a lot of hard work. I was DJing with negative equity – you weren't getting enough money to buy the records but you still did it because you did get some money and experience and you start doing weddings, roller discos, clubs where you had to wear a shirt and tie but eventually you break out of that. But if it's easy to get there then it's not rewarding anyway. And if it's difficult to get there and you still get there it means that you've got a strong heart."

Dave Clarke

The Bedroom DJ

"I DJ everywhere from Gateshead to John O'Groats. I didn't start out to be a DJ. I mean I always liked records. I always bought them with my paper-round money. For no money I'd selectively DJ at certain places. A stroke of luck was, there was a big R&B group and I did their party and I did Mary J Blige's at her concert. It's been hard work mainly – and a lot of hard work for nothing – but it pays off. I'd rather not have financial rewards, I'd rather be known as doing something. My advice to bedroom DJs out there is don't do it! No, it's good! It's nice to keep on top of things. Initially it was good fun but now it's actually work. You've obviously got to keep the tax man away, you have to work harder. Starting up is very difficult. My advice to people is basically work out your game plan. You don't have to be a good technical DJ – I'm not a good technical DJ. There's a lot of good turntablists out there who know how to give the crowd a good time and don't have an ego. The other thing about DJs is they disappear very quickly – so learn how to say please and thank you. I've been around for quite a while on the outskirts looking in and I've seen a lot of DJs disappear up their own backsides especially and a lot of it's because they have egos. They think they're the best, they spend more than they're getting in. Financially I'm a mess but I've learnt to be more sensible. It is a business. I've actually been sitting doing my tax returns today. And you don't have to be a music wizard – it's about having fun. And when the fun goes, get out. Pace yourself. Over the past five years I've done a Humanities Degree and I did quite well. I did my Masters this year and in two years' time I'm going to be a lecturer in Popular Culture."

Steve Sutherland, Galaxy FM DJ, winner of two MOBO Awards for
Best DJ

"Never leave your records in the car no matter how tired you are. If you are doing a club night and you have all your equipment in the back of your car unload it because I know so many people who lost all of their records that way. People know that you're a DJ and will help themselves. Know your equipment as well. Be interested in what goes on because if you turn up and you don't know how the mixer works ain't no one going to help you at the time. And the previous DJ will probably delight in watching you trying to work out which one is the cue button. I actually did a great one in my early days of working. I walked in and pressed a button and turned everything off. I'd turned the mixer off! Hang around DJ shops every so often! Read magazines. It's easy because most people have got Pioneers or Allen and Heath or Formula Sound. If you get to know those three mixers they all principally do the same but their cue buttons are in different places or their crossfader buttons or some have filters and it's just getting to know them. Go to work in lots of crappy clubs and bars. It's from that that I learnt how to fix mixers with bits of sellotape. So many DJs nowadays get fluff on their needles. It's something I've got into a habit of doing – just checking the needle beforehand. I nearly always take my own needles. You will turn up at crappy bars where they've just got two nails which will ruin your records. If you play somewhere decent then look at the needles and if they look good then leave them on if not you start fiddling."

Mark Doyle – Hed Kandi

"You do have to believe in yourself. That's why a lot of DJs are cocky. A lot of DJs are arrogant – it doesn't matter if they're famous or not because some of the most famous DJs are really nice, some of the nobodies are really arrogant. I knew that from working in a record store. But you do have to have a tiny bit of arrogance – maybe that's the wrong word – you have to be a bit cocky because you are controlling a whole atmosphere. It's not just you but you're a big part of it and you have to have guts. It's controlling your space. Sometimes people come up and stop the record – I just turn the music off and look at them. If I've a flashlight I point it right on them. They never do it again. One guy did once and I threw him out personally! As long as you're not a jerk and you don't put people down but if someone's messing with the music then they should be thrown out. Period!"

Cosmo

"With mixing you're trying to make two records sound as one and sound like they were naturally meant to be that way, so it's important that their key ranges are the same, the tempo's locked and the sounds complement each other. I always say you never have two bands playing their own music at their own tempos at the same time and doing their own thing in a mishmash. That's the whole aspect of playing records together and mixing and you don't have to be a DJ to know when someone's doing a terrible job! 'Damn! Why did he take the record out of there, I was really enjoying it!' "

Cutmaster Swift, DMC

"DJing can be an art form or just a bit of fun, but to me it's a whole way of life. I started DJing to escape problems at home and it changed my life. It gave me confidence, happiness and a wage! It's taken 10 years to get where I am today and I love it just as much as when it all began. It was a combination of 100 per cent dedication and a few lucky breaks and if it wasn't for my genuine love of music I might not have made it this far. It's a

166

tough game, and my advice to anyone is always the same, you can learn to mix but to make it as a professional DJ you have to love your music first and want the fame and glory second. Wanting the limelight alone, won't see you through."

Anne Savage

"There's people that break records and there's people that play hits and then there's those that do both. I try to do both but when you're starting out, play hits because you're not going to get away with trying to break records. Just play all the hits and it never goes wrong. And who cares if they say, 'I heard that record 20 million times.' There's the crowd going 'YEAHHHHH!' Nine out of 10 times you're going to be the only one to play the hits. You'll be the one in there not knowing how to mix and you're going to be playing all the hits. Everyone else will be like, 'I'm so cool, I just got the latest tunes and I'm gonna break these records in because this is what I like to play.' You'll be like, 'I've heard this record in five clubs and I'm gonna buy this record and play this record and it'll still be popular in a year's time when everyone has moved on.' What some DJs don't understand is that people crave to hear these records that were yesterday's records. It's cool to be on the edge but it's cool to have the edge and reminisce. Good music will never die. This is key to DJing and programming music. When they think they just had the ultimate record played, give them something they're not expecting, that they know is an ultimate record and then that's what makes you huge. If you're not a producer then start learning how to produce because it helps you in the long run if you have underground records. If you play house music then do funky house music. Get yourself involved in that area and you're playing your own records as well – you're starting to get a reputation. In DJ culture it takes both – the production side for you to build your reputation on the music that you play, and on the DJing side you have to have your craft. You don't have to be good. I've seen a lot of DJs that go out there and they're not good but they play great. They play great music but they don't blend great."

Ray Roc

"I think a good DJ plays from the heart, you need to feel a passion for what you are playing. Yes you need to able to mix properly, but if you are into what you are doing then this will come across in the tunes you play and the feeling you create in your set. I would say practise as much as you can at home but remember that you will be playing to a crowd so you need to keep them interested, it's no use just playing for yourself. Try to go record shopping at least once a week, keep on top of what is going on, be yourself, have your own style. Learn to use CDs as well and even add in your own effects and samples. Try to get some gigs so you can feel what it is like to play in front of a crowd, and above all enjoy."

Smokin' Jo

"The trick in succeeding I believe is not to follow a trend. Have faith in your own style, be yourself and play tracks you really love and believe in. It is also very important to remember to get that balance between originality and pleasing the crowd. I am extremely lucky to have a job I don't resent getting up for in the morning. It's a hobby and something I can make a living out of – I couldn't ask for more."

Paul Masterson (aka Yomanda/Hi-Gate)

"OK, firstly there is no such thing as a DJ 'career'. It is not something you can option as an A level. Almost all the successful DJs started long before there was the term 'clubland' and a DJ was considered somewhere between the glass collector and the cleaner in the staff at a 'discotheque'. I'm guessing but if you gathered the facts and did the sums you'd find the average DJ works for something like ten, that's TEN years before they even get paid more than the minimum. So any 20-year-old readers can expect to be 30 before anything happens. You work for free alongside other shitty jobs until by a combination of luck and circumstance you find you can give up the shitty jobs one by one until you are earning enough to live as a 'DJ'. One of the biggest myths is that DJs are rich. About 1 per cent of DJs are wealthy and maintaining that wealth leads you on a paper-round down Satan's driveway and right in his letterbox. The rest of us earn just enough. Honestly, mostly not enough. Then you take a shitty job again for a bit. Besides, no matter where you end up, talk to most DJs and they will moan constantly that they don't work enough or at the right places . . .

"There will never be 'superstar' DJs again. Occasional break-throughs like Lottie and Fergie are anomalies and only serve to fuel the wrong attitude to DJing, that you can become semi famous overnight. A DJ who does it for the right reasons wakes up and says, 'Today I want to play some records for people.' The wrong attitude is someone who wakes up and says, 'Today I want to be a DJ.' DJs are simply music lovers who like to show off a bit. It's not a career and the fact people get paid for it is an accident which has caused more ruination to the party than cocaine. Please note, I like money but I liked the innocence of Acid House more. Love music first, love careers, cars and maga-zine covers last."

Tim Sheridan

10

The Bedroom DJ

All too suddenly I found I had come to the end of my foray into the strange but beautiful world of DJing – or at least my initiation. What began as more or less a cathartic but perhaps childish attempt to exorcise the ghosts of my failed relationship and to get even with my ex was now ending with something deeper awakening in me. Could it be that the great DJ demon that troubled the ears of all the wonderful DJs I had been privileged enough to speak to – from scratching hero Cutmaster Swift to Mark Doyle of Hed Kandi and Roger Sanchez – be set to call upon little me? Only time would tell. Although talking to these professionals had dispelled many of the myths I had believed about how easy it was to become a DJ and what a life of luxury they were supposed to lead, the more I learned, the more intrigued I became and the more determined I was to do something with the enviable tuition I had received. I decided to set myself a new challenge.

As I write these lines I am busy organising a benefit club night for a London based charity. Blame Live Aid organiser and all-round saint Bob Geldof. Totally by accident I found myself engrossed in the former Boomtown Rat's autobiography *Is That It?* over the New Year when traditionally I start feeling guilty about my pointless selfish life anyway, my greedy record buying habits, pathetic desire to become the new Smokin' Jo and try to give up breathing or whatever the latest detox craze is. I was too young to really be familiar with much of the Rats' music. For example I was shocked by my appalling musical ignorance after learning that 'I Don't Like Mondays' was inspired by a young American woman who shot people dead from the window of her room simply because she was bored. I'd thought it was just about the fact that Bob didn't much like crawling out of bed of a Monday morning like the rest of us. Anyhow – the book fired my imagination.

Whereupon I decided a fundraising club night would kill two birds with one stone: salve my aching conscience and provide a fresh opportunity to try out my fledgling DJ skills in an environment less hostile than the invisible bar.

I am scared half to death, have no idea what I'm doing but have decided to hell with it, I'm doing it anyway. Cheekily I rang up a bar and somewhere along the line a miracle must have happened because the owner happily agreed to let me have the place for nothing for the night. He doesn't seem to realise that I haven't a clue how to organise a club night. What the hell have we let ourselves in for? Alastair and I are going to headline – under the imaginative monikers DJ Mullet and – yes you've guessed it – Bedroom DJ, although technically DJ Mullet is misleading as A mercifully cut off his mullet months ago after strict instructions from Nina. I *still* can't really mix properly, don't own anything like enough house records and worse still, A can't find his bag of treasured afrobeat records, which he thinks may have been stolen during our final suicidal night DJing down at the invisible bar. Despite the obvious fact staring us in the face that there wasn't a soul in the place who could possibly have pocketed them, unless it's the kleptomaniac ghost of the last DJ who died on his arse there before us.

Doing it all for 'charidee' adds that special edge of fear to my already churning stomach, because suddenly it isn't just a bedroom hobby anymore where it doesn't matter if no one turns up but our mums. Our future as DJs Mullet & Bedroom hangs in the balance. Will we rise to the occasion at our coming party, raise cash for the charity and fill the dancefloor or empty it as fast as a fart in an elevator? Only the elusive DJ demon knows for sure either way.

Information

COURSES:

DMC Ltd
PO Box 89
Slough
Berks
SL1 8NA
Tel: 01628 667124
E-mail: info@dmcworld.demon.com

Academy of Contemporary Music (ACM)
Guildford
www.acm.ac.uk
Tel: 01483 500 800

Point Blank
23–28 Penn Street
London
N1 5DL
E-mail: studio@point-blank.co.uk
www.point-blank.co.uk
Winner of DJ Magazine's course of the year award

VIDEOS:

So You Want To Be A DJ?
(Available from DMC. Everything you could ever need to
know about DJing in a handy visual format – including tips from
world-class DJs and studio technology)

The Art of Turntablism
(Cutmaster Swift, with the help of the Mixologists and Scratch Perverts, explains the history and techniques of scratching. Available from DMC)

DMC World Championships (Also available from DMC)

FURTHER READING:

How to DJ (Properly)
Frank Broughton & Bill Brewster (Bantam, 2002)
(What the Reader's Digest DIY book is to DJing – a great manual as long as you can endure the cringeworthy comparisons of bedroom DJing with wanking and playing to a crowd with promiscuity – and comes highly recommended by Sister Bliss)

Last Night a DJ Saved My Life – the History of the DJ
Frank Broughton & Bill Brewster (Headline, 1999)
(If you can take a deep breath and look beyond the comments in the introduction about female DJs being mostly rubbish, this is a stirling history and celebration of the disc jockey from the days of Sir Jimmy Saville to Grandmaster Flash and Kool Herc)

Pump Up The Volume
Sean Bidder (Channel 4, 2001)
(Druggy but insightful history of dance music as seen – not always that clearly – by those who lived through it)

WEBSITES:

htfr.co.uk
(hard to find records)
(as its names suggests – good for tracking down those tricky record buys as well as equipment and accessories)

Information

DMCworld.com
(The website of the worldwide DJ organisation – a must for all
DJs – bedroom or otherwise)

MAGAZINES (from all good newsagents – dunno about
the bad ones though!)

Jockey Slut

DJ Magazine

Musik Magazine

Mixmag

The Source

Vibe